中国古典文学英译丛书

竹林七贤诗赋英译

Selected Poetic Writings of the Seven Worthies of the Bamboo Grove

〔美〕吴伏生 〔英〕格雷厄姆·哈蒂尔 编译

Translated by Wu Fusheng and Graham Hartill

商务印书馆
The Commercial Press

2020年·北京

图书在版编目(CIP)数据

竹林七贤诗赋英译/(美)吴伏生,(英)格雷厄姆·哈蒂尔(Graham Hartill)编译.—北京:商务印书馆,2020
(中国古典文学英译丛书)
ISBN 978-7-100-18346-8

Ⅰ.①竹… Ⅱ.①吴…②格… Ⅲ.①古典诗歌—诗集—中国—魏晋南北朝时代—汉、英 Ⅳ.①I222.735

中国版本图书馆 CIP 数据核字(2020)第 068125 号

权利保留,侵权必究。

中国古典文学英译丛书
竹林七贤诗赋英译
〔美〕吴伏生 〔英〕格雷厄姆·哈蒂尔 编译

商务印书馆出版
(北京王府井大街36号 邮政编码100710)
商务印书馆发行
北京市十月印刷有限公司印刷
ISBN 978-7-100-18346-8

2020年6月第1版 开本880×1240 1/32
2020年6月北京第1次印刷 印张 8¾
定价:45.00元

目 录
Contents

前言　Introduction ·· 1

阮 籍
Ruan Ji

咏怀诗选　Selections from *Songs of My Heart* ·············· 24

嵇 康
Ji Kang

秋胡行七章　A Qiu Hu Song (in seven stanzas) ············ 150
幽愤诗　Pent-up Sorrow ·································· 164
四言赠兄秀才入军十八章　A Tetrasyllabic Poem on Seeing Off My Brother the Cultivated Talent to Join the Army (in eighteen stanzas) ·································· 174
五言赠秀才诗　A Pentasyllabic Poem to My Brother the Cultivated Talent ·································· 210
酒会诗　A Party Poem ·································· 214
述志诗二首　Expressing My Will: Two Poems ············ 216
答二郭三首　In Reply to the Two Guos: Three Poems ······ 224
与阮德如　To Ruan Deru ·································· 236

四言诗	Tetrasyllabic Verses	240
思亲诗	Missing My Loved Ones	248
六言诗	Hexasyllabic Verses	252
东方朔至清	Dongfang Shuo, The Ultimate Purity	252
老莱妻贤名	Lao Lai's Wife, A Virtuous Name	254
嗟古贤原宪	In Praise of the Ancient Worthy Yuan Xian	256

向 秀
Xiang Xiu

思旧赋（并序） Rhapsody on Recalling Old Friends (with a Preface) ⋯⋯ 260

刘 伶
Liu Ling

北芒客舍诗 Sojourning at Beimang Mountain ⋯⋯ 266
酒德颂 Ode to the Virtue of Wine ⋯⋯ 268

译者简介 About the Translators ⋯⋯ 272

前　言

　　竹林七贤是指魏晋时期名重一时的七位士人，他们是阮籍（210—263）、嵇康（224—263）、山涛（205—283）、刘伶（？—？）、阮咸（？—？）向秀（227—272）及王戎（234—305）。有关他们一起为"竹林之游"的记载虽然不少，但大都是只言片语，缺少细节。其中最早、最详细的，便是于刘宋期间成书的《世说新语·任诞》篇中的如下文字，即此七人"常集于竹林之下，肆意酣畅，故世谓竹林七贤"。值得注意的是，此处所提及的交游内容，只有"肆意酣畅"。的确，竹林七贤各成员之间在年龄、性格、志向方面都有不小的差异，他们所选择的人生道路也大相径庭。魏晋时期正值司马氏以晋代魏、改朝换代之际，朝廷中不同派系相互倾轧，政治斗争异常惨烈，使得当时"名士少有全者"（《晋书·阮籍传》）。面对这种境遇，嵇康在权贵面前傲骨凛然，而且为保持清风亮节，不惜与劝其出仕的友人山涛绝交，最终为当权者所害。刘伶、阮咸寝身隐迹，致使后代不知其生年卒月。阮籍、向秀与当权者屈身妥协，得以苟全。山涛、王戎则在仕途上青云直上，位至司徒。尤其是王戎，虽然身居高位，享尽荣华富贵，却以"俭啬"闻名，因女儿借钱不还而耿耿于怀,甚至钻核卖李;《世说新语·俭啬》篇共九节,竟有四节涉及王戎。如此陋行,真是与竹林七贤在后代读者心目中的形象格格不入。不仅如此,竹林七贤虽常在一起"肆意酣畅",但似乎并未如当时士人通常所做的那样,因文会友,以诗相酬。现存嵇康诗中很多是赠答诗,但其对象却没有七贤当中的任何一员。嵇康有一首《酒会诗》,但从其首句"乐哉苑中游"来看,所描写的也不是那为人称道的"竹林之游",而是多为当时士人所歌咏的"公宴"。总之,"竹林七贤"这一称呼听上去似乎蕴含深广,令人肃然起敬,但一旦探究,我们便会发现它盛名之下,其实难副。

七贤当中,山涛、王戎、阮咸都没有为后代留下任何诗作。因此,现在我们所呈现给读者的这本《竹林七贤诗赋选英译》,只包含其余四位的作品,其中向秀只有一篇,刘伶有两篇。阮籍、嵇康作为竹林七贤的领袖,不仅在任性独往、蔑视礼法方面身体力行,而且在诗文创作上也倾心注目,成果斐然,在当时乃至整个中国文学史上都是为人称道的大家。为此,我们这个选本所收录的,基本上也都是这两位诗人的作品。有关上述四位诗人的生平事迹,书中各节开始略有介绍,兹不赘述。

早在南北朝时期,阮籍和嵇康的诗歌便引起了人们的关注。钟嵘(约468—约518)在其《诗品》中分别把他们列入上、中二品。下面是他对阮籍诗歌的评价:

其源出于小雅,无雕虫之功。而咏怀之作,可以陶性灵，发幽思。言在耳目之内，情寄八荒之表，洋洋乎会于风雅。使人忘其鄙近，自致远大，颇多感慨之词。厥旨渊放，归趣难求。

在钟嵘看来，阮诗在源流体制、抒情言志、陶冶性情方面都可谓雅正完备，感人至深。除此之外，他还特别指出了阮诗含蓄蕴藉的风格，即"厥旨渊放，归趣难求"。钟嵘认为，诗歌的极致，便是要产生出一种"滋味"，并"使咏之者无极，闻之者动心"（《诗品·序》）。若欲达到这一境界，则须赋、比、兴并用。他对这三种手法的定义是："文已尽而意有余，兴也；因物喻志，比也；直书其事，寓言写物，赋也。"（《诗品·序》）阮籍的很多诗篇便多采用这些手法，并且把它们锤炼到了炉火纯青的程度。下面便是《咏怀》组诗中的第一首：

夜中不能寐，起坐弹鸣琴。
薄帷鉴明月，清风吹我襟。
孤鸿号外野，翔鸟鸣北林。
徘徊将何见，忧思独伤心。

诗的前两行直接描绘诗人的状况，是赋。接下来中间四行都是比兴，借此引入外界物象，令它们与诗人及其心灵相互作用，进而达到二者浑然一体，水乳不分。最后两行表面上看似乎是再度采用赋法，直接倾述诗人内心的"忧思"，但诗人并未对此做任何解说；不仅如此，由于前面的铺垫与烘托，这一忧思已经变得与诗中的各个比兴意象互为表里，难分难解。如此形成的"滋味"或意旨，自然是"渊放"与"难求"。再如下面这一首（《咏怀诗·十四》）：

> 开秋肇凉气，蟋蟀鸣床帷。
> 感物怀殷忧，悄悄令心悲。
> 多言焉所告，繁辞将诉谁。
> 微风吹罗袂，明月耀清晖。
> 晨鸡鸣高树，命驾起旋归。

虽然此诗展开的顺序与前一首不同，即它以比兴开始，继以"感悟"抒怀，又终以比兴，但其回旋往复的效果完全相同，即虽然诗中弥漫着一种"悲"情，但读者对此只能体味，却无法坐实。

与此相比，钟嵘对嵇康的诗歌则颇有微词：

> 颇似魏文，过为峻切，讦直露才，伤渊雅之致。然托喻清远，良有鉴裁，亦未失高流矣。

钟嵘把阮诗溯源到《诗经》中的小雅，正是要确立其经典地位。此处他认为嵇诗滥觞于同被他列为中品的魏文帝曹丕，其评价态度也不言自明。虽然如此，钟嵘用"讦直露才，伤渊雅之致"如此激烈的语言对之进行指摘，仍然令人未免为之一惊，因为在六朝时期，嵇康已经是令人崇敬的高士。必须指出的是，嵇康诗歌中四言居多，而钟嵘则认为四言诗"文繁而意少",五言诗则"居文词之要,是众作之有滋味者也"(《诗品·序》)。如此态度,自然要影响到他对嵇康诗歌的评价。但是,纵观嵇康的诗歌,我们难免感到他不时在诗中议论说理。刘勰(约465—约532)在《文心雕龙·才略》篇中曾对阮籍和嵇康做过比较。他说:"嵇康师心以遣论,阮籍使气以命诗。"刘勰此处所说的,固然是嵇康以论说文而名、阮籍因抒情诗而显这一历史现象,因而尽管有此区别,二人仍然"殊声而合响,异翮而同飞",在文、诗领域各领风骚。但是,嵇康时常将"论"引入"诗"中,则是事实。这也便是钟嵘批评嵇诗"讦直露才,伤渊雅之致"的原因。例如其《述志诗》第二首:

> 斥鷃擅蒿林,仰笑神凤飞。
> 坎井蜻蛙宅,神龟安所归。
> 恨自用身拙,任意多永思。
> 远实与世殊,义誉非所希。
> 往事既已谬,来者犹可追。
> 何为人事间,自令心不夷。
> 慷慨思古人,梦想见容辉。
> 愿与知己遇,舒愤启其微。
> 岩穴多隐逸,轻举求吾师。
> 晨登箕山巅,日夕不知饥。
> 玄居养营魄,千载长自绥。

前四行采用比兴,通过"斥鷃"与"神凤"、"蜻蛙"与"神龟"之间的对比，象征诗人超尘脱俗的情怀，并引发其"恨自用身拙，任意多永思"的认识与感叹；诗的其余部分则采用赋法对上述主题以及对策进行铺陈与解说，并以"玄居养营魄，千载长自绥"作为总结与自励，使得读者对诗中的主题一目了然，体会不到"咏之无极"的余兴。虽然诗中所抒发的疾世隐逸情怀令人敬仰，但从艺术的角度来衡量，毕竟有所缺憾。钟嵘把诗歌创作视为一种艺术（"诗之为技"《诗品·序》），尤其强调诗意要"咏之无极"，他对嵇诗的批评，正是以此为基点。

如上所述，嵇康诗歌的主要成就，体现在其四言诗中。他是继曹操之后刻意从事四言诗写作的少数大诗人之一。下面便是一首代表作：

> 息徒兰圃，秣马华山。
> 流磻平皋，垂纶长川。
> 目送归鸿，手挥五弦。
> 俯仰自得，游心太玄。
> 嘉彼钓叟，得鱼忘筌。
> 郢人逝矣，谁与尽言？

此为《四言赠兄秀才入军十八章》组诗中的第十四节。四言诗源自《诗经》，极难脱离其窠臼，后人采用，往往给人以艰涩古板之感；将其用于仪式或官场固然得体，但用来抒情则未免拘束。嵇康此诗则流畅清丽，因为它不但没有用一个三百篇的典故，而且基本排除了其所惯用词汇。尤其是

"目送归鸿，手挥五弦"两句，生动地描述了诗人在自然与艺术中物我两忘的境界，句法对仗工整，措辞近乎白描，但却形象鲜明，意味无穷，成为千古绝唱。

在汉诗翻译中，历来有韵体与素体之争。我们采用的是素体自由诗，因为我们认为它更能体现原诗的意义和意境。美国现代派诗人、诗歌翻译家庞德（Ezra Pound, 1885—1972）曾说过，任何诗歌都有可译与不可译的成分。诗歌的音乐、格律无法从原语转换到译语，但诗歌的内容和意象则是可以转换的。他还认为，构成诗歌的精华，便是可译的内容和意象。[1]我们非常认同这一观点。翻译，尤其是诗歌翻译，难免会导致原作某些特色的流失。面对这种情况，尽量准确地翻译原诗中的意义和意象，总比试图翻译原诗中不可再现的音韵格律更为明智可取。另外，庞德的好友，诗人与批评家艾略特（T. S. Eliot, 1888—1965）也曾指出，"每一个时代都必须为自己翻译"[2]，也就是说，诗歌翻译应该具有时代特征。在当今英美诗坛，自由诗早已成为诗人创作的主要诗体和译者译诗的主要形式。为此，我们认为诗歌翻译采用自由诗体不仅行之有效，也是大势所趋，因为它更能体现当今英美诗歌的时代精神以及读者的审美取向。

在编译这个选本时，我们主要参考了逯钦立的《先秦汉

---

[1] "French Poets," in *Little Review*, IV, 10 (February, 1918)。另请参见吴伏生《汉诗英译研究：理雅各、翟理斯、韦利、庞德》（北京：学苑出版社，2012年），第339页。

[2] "Each generation must translate for itself." 此语出自艾略特为庞德汉诗翻译所写的序言；参见 Ezra Pound: *New Selected Poems and Translations*, edited by Richard Sieburth, New York: New Directions, 2010, p. 367.

魏晋南北朝诗》(中华书局,1983)、陈伯君的《阮籍集校注》(中华书局,1987)、戴明扬的《嵇康集校注》(中华书局,1962)、韩格平的《竹林七贤诗文全集译注》(吉林文史出版社,1997),以及萧统的《文选》等著作。此处,我们要再次感谢商务印书馆和许晓娟编辑。能够与商务印书馆长期合作,翻译古诗,我们感到莫大的荣幸与欣慰。

吴伏生　Graham Hartill
2018年春

Introduction

The Seven Worthies of the Bamboo Grove refers to seven renowned literati of the Wei-Jin dynasties era; they are Ruan Ji (210–263), Ji Kang (224–263), Shan Tao (205–283), Liu Ling (?–?), Ruan Xian (?–?), Xiang Xiu (227–272), and Wang Rong (234–305). Although not a few historical sources make mention of their "bamboo grove excursions," they never provide meaningful details and hence remain tantalizingly elusive. The earliest, most detailed of these is an account in the "Free and Unrestrained" chapter of Liu Yiqing's (403–444) *A New Account of Tales of the World*, that they "often gathered under a bamboo grove, let loose themselves and drank heartily; because of this people at that time called them 'Seven Worthies of the Bamboo Grove.' " It is noteworthy that in this account the only activity that is mentioned is "letting loose themselves and drinking heartily." Indeed, the seven people here, although named together under a common label, were very different in age, character, ambition, and they made very different choices in their lives and careers as well. During the period in question, the Sima clan had begun the process of replacing the Wei dynasty with the Jin, and there were fierce factional struggles in the court. Many people lost their lives, to the extent that "few renowned literati survived intact." Faced with this historical change and political danger, Ji Kang chose to stand up against the authorities; moreover, in order to preserve his honor and integrity, he even cut off his friendship with Shan Tao when the latter recommended Ji Kang to take up a position in the government. For this defiance Ji Kang later paid the ultimate price. Liu Ling and Ruan Xian opted to hide themselves, so that posterity didn't even know the years of their birth and death. Ruan Ji and Xiang Xiu made compromises with the authorities, thereby managing to survive. Shan Tao and Wang Rong had a smooth ride in their official careers and rose all the way to ministry-level positions. Wang Rong, in particular, was also known as a "stingy and mean" person; of the nine episodes in the "Stinginess and Meanness" chapter in the *A New Account of the Tales of the World*, four are about his stingy and mean conduct, even toward his own daughter because she did not return in time the money she borrowed from her father. In short, the seven members of this historically renowned bamboo-grove club are in fact very different people. When we look into their literary activities, we encounter another lacuna. Unlike the Seven Masters of the Jian'an era who feasted and composed poems together, the Seven Worthies of the Bamboo

Grove did not leave any writing that resulted from their famed gatherings beneath the bamboo grove. In the poetic output of Ji Kang, for example, many are poetic exchanges between him and friends/colleagues, but none is addressed to one of the seven worthies. One of his poems is titled "A Party Poem," but judging from its opening line, "Happily we roam and saunter in the park," we may infer that what is being described is not their famed excursion to the bamboo grove, but one of those "lordly parties" that often feature in the poems of the period. In sum, the label "Seven Worthies of the Bamboo Grove" may conjure up in reader's mind lofty associations of noble-minded scholars engaged in free and carefree drinking, sauntering and writing, but when we endeavor to substantiate these associations with historical findings, we are left with an acute sense of disappointment.

Of the seven worthies, Shan Tao, Wang Rong, and Ruan Xian did not leave behind any poetic works, so this *Selected Poetic Writings of the Seven Worthies* is in fact comprised of the poems and rhapsodies of the other four. Since Xiang Xiu and Liu Ling each only has one and two extant pieces respectively, this selection contains mainly the poems of Ruan Ji and Ji Kang. A short biographical sketch of each of the four poets is provided at the beginning of his section.

Ruan Ji and Ji Kang were not only the most prominent members of the Seven Worthies, they were also among the greatest poets in the Chinese poetic tradition. As early as the fifth and sixth centuries, critics had begun to treat their poetry as major contributions to the canon. Zhong Rong (ca. 468–ca. 518) classified their poetry into the first and second ranks respectively in his influential work, *The Ranking of Poetry*. Here are his comments on Ruan Ji's poetry:

> They originate from the Small Elegantiae [of *The Book of Poetry*], and do not show the workmanship of insect carving. His *Songs of My Heart* can nourish our soul and convey deep thought. Their words may fall within the range of our ears and eyes, but their sentiment reaches the edge of each of the eight wilds, merging profusely with the Songs and Elegantiaes [of *The Book of Poetry*]. They make us forget what is mean and close-by to us, so we may try our best to aim at what is far and great. Their meaning is profoundly broad, and their significance is hard to pin down.

In Zhong Rong's opinion, Ruan Ji's poetry is graceful and balanced in its origin, format, and expressiveness; it has the capacity to nourish our souls and move our hearts. In addition, he also points out the subtle reservedness that is the hallmark of Ruan Ji's poetic style, that its "meaning is profoundly broad, and its significance is hard to pin down." Zhong Rong also proposes that the ultimate success in poetry is to produce a "flavor," so that "those who chant it have no limit [in their experience], and those who hear it have their hearts stirred." In order to arrive at this state, a poet must utilize all three rhetorical devices embodied in *The Book of Poetry*, namely exposition, comparison, and evocation. Zhong Rong also offers his new definition of these three devices:

> When words have come to their end but meaning remains lingering, we have evocation; when one conveys his intent by the means of things, we have comparison; when one directly describes an event, entrusts words to depict an object, we have exposition.

Many of Ruan Ji's poems demonstrate fully the effectiveness of these devices. The following is the opening poem of his eighty-two *Songs of My Heart* series:

夜中不能寐，	Midnight, and I can't sleep,
起坐弹鸣琴。	sitting up, I play upon my zither.
薄帷鉴明月，	My gauze curtains mirror the moonlight,
清风吹我襟。	fresh breeze, fluttering my sleeves.
孤鸿号外野，	The lone swan cries, crossing the wilderness,
翔鸟鸣北林。	flying birds shriek from the northern wood.
徘徊将何见？	Pacing the courtyard, pacing the courtyard, what can I see?
忧思独伤心。	Only anxiety, fretting my heart.

The first two lines directly portray the poet's current condition, hence they are exposition. The next four lines are comparison and evocation, whereby the poet includes external images such as the moon, wind, birds, and have them interact with him, creating a state where the man and his surroundings are blended into each other. The last two lines seem to again employ exposition because they describe the poet's physical act of pacing and state his feeling of sadness, but since by then this sadness has been so informed by the images in the previous part of the poem, it becomes virtually impossible to separate them, just as it is very hard to separate exposition, with its non-metaphorical directness, from comparison and evocation, with their metaphorical indirectness, in this poem. The result is a "profoundly broad" meaning or "flavor," which, because it results from a fusion of different components of the poem, refuses to be pinned down into a single category.

Poem 14 displays similar qualities, albeit in a slightly different manner:

十四	14
开秋肇凉气，	Autumn: I know that it's going to be cold,
蟋蟀鸣床帷。	lying in bed, listening to the cricket sing
感物怀殷忧，	the other side of the curtain. I am fearful,
悄悄令心悲。	saddened by this little natural thing.
多言焉所告，	A swelling heart, with whom to share?

繁辞将诉谁。	A sea of words, with whom to speak?
微风吹罗袂，	Gently the breeze tugs at my silken sleeves.
明月耀清晖。	The moon is bright, it shines like ice.
晨鸡鸣高树，	I hear the cockerel crow in the tree-top
命驾起旋归。	and order my horse to be saddled. Time to return.

The first two lines employ metaphorical language (evocation and comparison); the middle four lines are direct articulation of the poet's sentiment (exposition); the final four lines revert back to the metaphorical mode. As in the earlier poem, this piece is also permeated with a feeling of sadness, which, because of its blending various rhetorical devices and imagistic qualities, remains hauntingly present but elusive.

Ji Kang's poetry did not receive similar praise from Zhong Rong. As mentioned earlier, Zhong Rong assigned Ji Kang's poetry to the second rank; his following remark in *The Ranking of Poetry* provides an explanation for this judgement:

[His poetry] very much resembles that of Emperor Wen. It is too harsh, full of direct critiques in order to show off his own natural ability, causing harm to what is deep and graceful. Nonetheless, it embodies a clear and far-reaching quality, often displaying sound judgement; it thus deserves to be placed together with what is lofty.

Zhong Rong has traced Ruan Ji's poetry to the Small Elegantiae section of *The Book of Poetry* in order to give it a prominent position in the Chinese canon. Here, not only does he rank Ji Kang's poetry lower, he also assigns it a much less canonical and authoritative source, the poetry of Cao Pi, Emperor Wen of the Wei dynasty (r. 220–226), which is also placed in the middle rank by Zhong Rong in the same book. This critical attitude is further demonstrated by his startlingly severe criticism of Ji Kang's poetry, that it is "too harsh, full of direct critiques in order to show off his own natural ability, causing harm to what is deep and graceful." This is startling because by Zhong Rong's time Ji Kang had become an icon for the lofty disdain of authority. It should be noted that most of Ji Kang's poetry is cast in the four-character line format, but in Zhong Rong's opinion, the best poetic format is the five-character line, because it is the one that has the most "flavor." In comparison, four-character line poetry is "wordy but lacks meaning." Indeed, Ji Kang's poetry has a didactic quality that might have put off Zhong Rong. Another renowned critic of the time, Liu Xie (ca. 465–ca. 532), the author of *The Literary Mind and Carving of Dragons*, also made a comparison of Ruan Ji and Ji Kang. His words are: "Ji Kang follows his mind to give out critiques, Ruan Ji utilizes his energy to write poetry." Liu Xie may be referring to the fact that Ji Kang is better known for his discursive writing in prose, whereas Ruan Ji is regarded as a master of poetry, but his remark does reveal a concern that Ji Kang often injects a discursive and didactic element into his poetry, which, according to Zhong Rong, causes harm to "what is deep and graceful" that he admires so much in Ruan Ji's poetry. For an illustration of this, let us take a look at the following poem:

述志诗二首   Expressing My Will: Two Poems
二   2

斥鷃擅蒿林，	Quails have taken control of wormwood bushes,
仰笑神凤飞。	they laugh at the soaring godly phoenix.
坎井蝤蛙宅，	Beetles and frogs reside in shallow wells,
神龟安所归？	where will the godly turtle find his place?
恨自用身拙，	I regret the awkward way I conduct myself;
任意多永思。	often I am too thoughtful and stubborn.
远实与世殊，	Far from reality, removed from the world,
义誉非所希。	I care little for righteousness and fame.
往事既已谬，	Mistakes have been made in the past,
来者犹可追。	yet I still have hopes for the future.
何为人事间，	Why must I fret about worldly affairs,
自令心不夷？	making my heart so ill at ease?
慷慨思古人，	In deepest thought I turn to the ancients,
梦想见容辉。	and long for a glimpse of their brilliant faces.
愿与知己遇，	I wish to meet with an understanding friend,

舒愤启其微。	to relieve my distress and share his mystery.
岩穴多隐逸，	Rocks and caves attract many a hermit,
轻举求吾师。	I would fly there to seek my masters.
晨登箕山巅，	I would ascend Mount Ji in the morning,
日夕不知饥。	and even at dusk I would feel no hunger.
玄居养营魄，	I would hide in the darkness to nourish my soul,
千载长自绥。	and to live in peace for a thousand years!

The first four lines adopt the metaphorical devices of comparison and evocation, in order to introduce the poem's topic, a self-realization by the poet that "I regret the awkward way I conduct myself,/ often I am too thoughtful and stubborn," namely, he is, like the phoenix and godly turtle, out of step with the world. The rest of the poem discourses, at some length, on this dilemma and the poet's plans to address it, that "I would hide in the darkness to nourish my soul,/and to live in peace for a thousand years!" The result is that by the end of the poem the reader is given an exhausted explication of its theme; there is little remaining "flavor" left for him to savor. Although the eremitic sentiment expressed therein is lofty and inspiring, it has been subjected to a rational dissection that nearly "murders" it. For Zhong Rong, who regards poetry as a kind of "art" and who values a lingering "flavor," this type of poetry leaves much to be desired.

As has been noted earlier, Ji Kang's main poetic achievement lies in his four-character line poetry. After Cao Cao, he is one of the few masters of this poetic form. The following is an example:

息徒兰圃，	We take a rest on the violet field,
秣马华山。	and feed our horses along the flowery hill.
流磻平皋，	We shoot arrows across the moor,
垂纶长川。	cast our lines on the long stream.
目送归鸿，	My eyes see off the returning geese,
手挥五弦。	my fingers pluck the five-stringed zither.
俯仰自得，	Up and down, to my heart's content,
游心太玄。	I let my mind roam through the Great Mystery.
嘉彼钓叟，	How greatly I honor that fisherman
得鱼忘筌。	who, catching the fish, forgets the trap.
郢人逝矣，	The man from Ying is gone forever,
谁与尽言？	with whom can I share my words again?

This is the fourteenth stanza of his long poem, "A Tetrasyllabic Poem on Seeing Off My Brother the Cultivated Talent to Join the Army" (in eighteen stanzas). The four-character line, or tetrasyllabic verse, originates from *The Book of Poetry*, which, because of its canonical status, often exerts a confining influence upon later poets. By Ji Kang's time, poems cast in this mold often sound archaic and stilted; although it might suit well formal and ritual occasions, but when employed for personal expression, it could cause difficulties and even obstacles. Ji Kang's verse, however, demonstrates a remarkable ease and clarity. It does not use a single allusion to *The Book of Poetry*, and by and large avoids its diction and phrases. The following two lines, "My eyes see off the returning geese,/ my fingers pluck the five-stringed zither," present a vivid description of the poet immersed in his communion with nature and art, an ideal state in Chinese philosophy. This is further demonstrated by the skillful yet natural deployment of language: although these two lines are cast in parallelism, they do not betray a trace of artificiality; instead, the rhetorical device helps to emphasize the integration and harmony between the poet, nature, and art. Small wonder that these two lines are among the most beloved in Chinese poetry.

In poetry translation there have always been two different approaches: rhymed translation versus unrhymed translation. We have adopted unrhymed free verse in our translation because we believe that this method can produce better translations of Chinese poems. Ezra Pound (1855–1972), who himself was a poet and translator of poetry, once remarked that in poetry translation music and metrical pattern in the original cannot be translated. He further noted that what constitutes the core of poetry is what can be translated into another language, namely content and imagery.[1] We agree

---

1 See his "French Poets," in *Little Review*, IV, 10 (February, 1918).

with this view. Translation, especially poetry translation, inevitably will incur the loss of certain features in the original. Faced with this dilemma, it is certainly wiser to concentrate on translating what can be translated, namely the content and imagery of the original, rather than to attempt at rendering its musical quality and metrical pattern, which are unique to each individual language and hence are next to impossible to replicate in a foreign tongue. Moreover, as Pound's friend, the renowned poet and critic T. S. Eliot (1888–1965) once pointed out, "Each generation must translate for itself."[1] In other words, in translating poetry a translator must aim to manifest the poetic aspirations of his/her time. At the moment, free verse has long become the main style for both poetic composition and translation in the English-speaking world. For this reason, we believe that adopting free verse in translating Chinese poetry is not only more effective, but can better represent the current trends of English poetry and the aesthetic inclination of its readers.

In putting together this selection, we have consulted Lu Qinli's *The Poetry of the Pre-Qin, Han, Wei, Jin and Northern-Southern Dynasties* (Beijing: Zhonghua Book Company, 1983), Chen Bojun's *Annotated Collection of Ruan Ji's Works* (Beijing: Zhonghua Book Company, 1987), Dai Mingyang's *Annotated*

---

1 In *Ezra Pound: New Selected Poems and Translations*, edited by Richard Sieburth. New York: New Directions, 2010, p. 367.

Collection of Ji Kang's Works (Beijing: Zhonghua Book Company, 1962), Han Geping's *Annotated and Translated Collection of the Writings by the Seven Worthies of the Bamboo Grove* (Changchun: Jilin Literature and History Press, 1997), and *Selections of Refined Literature* by Xiao Tong. Once more we would like to express our gratitude to Ms. Xu Xiaojuan of the Commercial Press. Thanks to her support, we have the honor and privilege to continue translating classical Chinese poetry for her prestigious press.

Wu Fusheng and Graham Hartill
Spring, 2018

阮 籍

Ruan Ji

阮籍(210—263),字嗣宗,建安七子之一阮瑀之子,魏晋之交著名士人。他曾有过济世之志,但生逢乱世,面对朝廷残酷的政治斗争与迫害,只得选择佯狂避世。他任性独往,蔑视礼法,虽在朝廷及地方担任过多职,但遗落世事,以饮酒赋诗、登山临水为乐,最终得以全身。所作八十二首咏怀诗,充满了忧患意识以及对自由世界的追求,始终被视为中国诗歌的典范。

Ruan Ji (210-263), courtesy name Sizong, was the son of Ruan Yu, one of the Seven Masters of the Jian'an era, and a renowned literatus of his own time. He had wanted to avail himself to the world, but the chaos of the time forced him to feign an escapism in order to stay out of the dangerous power struggles and persecutions in the court. Fiercely independent by nature, he disdained laws and rituals, and although he served in various positions in the central and local governments, he chose to be disengaged and devoted his time to drinking, writing and roaming instead. This attitude and strategy enabled him to survive intact the chaos and danger of the time. His eighty-two poems entitled *Songs of My Heart* teem with deeply-felt personal, social anxieties and passionate longing for freedom; they have always been regarded as a model for Chinese poetry.

咏怀诗选

一

夜中不能寐,
起坐弹鸣琴。
薄帷鉴明月,
清风吹我襟。
孤鸿号外野,
翔鸟鸣北林。
徘徊将何见?
忧思独伤心。

Selections from *Songs of My Heart*[1]

1

Midnight, and I can't sleep,

sitting up, I play upon my zither.

My gauze curtains mirror the moonlight,

fresh breeze, fluttering my sleeves.

The lone swan cries, crossing the wilderness,

flying birds shriek from the northern wood.

Pacing the courtyard, pacing the courtyard,
what can I see?

Only anxiety, fretting my heart.

Ruan Ji

---
1 八十二选六十。Sixty out of eighty-two.

二

二妃游江滨,
逍遥顺风翔。
交甫怀环佩,
婉娈有芬芳。
猗靡情欢爱,
千载不相忘。
倾城迷下蔡,
容好结中肠。
感激生忧思,
萱草树兰房,
膏沐为谁施,
其雨怨朝阳。
如何金石交,
一旦更离伤。

阮籍
26

2

Two fairy maidens played along the riverbank,

lightly, leisurely, hanging on the wind.

They gave their beautiful jewelry to Jiaofu,

how he treasured its fragrance!

Jiaofu and the maidens fell deeply in love

and swore they would never forget one another.

These maidens charmed the entire town,

Their beauty made its people enchanted.

Alas! Their love, and their gratitude, turned to anxiety,

soon they were planting forgetful herbs before their chambers.

So what's the use of putting on make-up?

Hope for rain is dashed by the morning sun.

Gold-stone and companionship –

one day they will both dissolve.

Ruan Ji

三

嘉树下成蹊，
东园桃与李。
秋风吹飞藿，
零落从此始。
繁华有憔悴，
堂上生荆杞。
驱马舍之去，
去上西山趾。
一身不自保，
何况恋妻子。
凝霜被野草，
岁暮亦云已。

3

Under the fine trees, paths have taken shape,

in the Eastern Garden – peaches, plum trees,

bean-leaves flying everywhere, Autumn wind.

But from now on, everything withers and dies.

Blooming flowers will one day shrivel,

thorns and weeds sprout in the courtyard.

Time to mount my horse, to leave it all,

and head for the West Mountain:[1]

when you can't be sure of your own security

how can you care for your wife and children?

Frost thickens the wild grass,

the year grows old – there's no more left to say.

---

1 西山为商末伯夷、叔齐隐身之地。West Mountain was where ancient hermits Boyi and Shuqi went to hide themselves at the end of the Shang dynasty.

五

平生少年时,
轻薄好弦歌。
西游咸阳中,
赵李相经过。
娱乐未终极,
白日忽蹉跎。
驱马复来归,
反顾望三河。
黄金百镒尽,
资用常苦多。
北临太行道,
失路将如何?

5

I remember when I was young at heart,

I paid no heed, singing and playing.

Off I went west to Xianyang, the capital,

there to tease the women, flirt with the rich.

All this pleasure was still at its height

when suddenly, night-time fell.

Now I return, on horseback,

and gaze across the far reaches of Three Rivers.

Hundreds of pounds of gold may be wasted –

never mind. We suffer from too much wealth.

Before me the road runs away to the north;

how can I find the way to my lost road?

六

昔闻东陵瓜,
近在青门外。
连畛距阡陌,
子母相钩带。
五色曜朝日,
嘉宾四面会。
膏火自煎熬,
多财为患害。
布衣可终身,
宠禄岂足赖?

6

I've heard that where the recluse Dongling used to live
he planted melons, right up to the city gates,
so thickly, they covered the earth,
mothers and children, clinging together, spilling across the paths.
The morning sun would dazzle from them so,
that noble guests would come from all over the country
to gather among their brilliant colors.
Alas, the oil-lamp burns, and consumes only itself,
and too much wealth is a burden, bringing disaster.
All my life I have wanted to wear only the most humble clothes;
how can we let ourselves depend on fortune and rank?

七

炎暑惟兹夏，
三旬将欲移。
芳树垂绿叶，
青云自逶迤。
四时更代谢，
日月递差驰。
徘徊空堂上，
忉怛莫我知。
愿睹卒欢好，
不见悲别离。

7

This sweltering heat will take its leave of us,

the summer months will not want to stay.

Fragrant trees, heavy with bright leaves,

blue clouds, wandering across the sky...

So the four seasons turn, and turn around,

the Sun and the Moon rise and fall in succession.

Back and forth I pace the empty courtyard,

nobody but myself to behold my sadness.

I hope in the end for happiness, and harmony,

not pain, not separation.

八

灼灼西隤日,
余光照我衣。
回风吹四壁,
寒鸟相因依。
周周尚衔羽,
蛩蛩亦念饥,
如何当路子,
磬折忘所归!
岂为夸与名?
憔悴使心悲。
宁与燕雀翔,
不随黄鹄飞。
黄鹄游四海,
中路将安归?

8

The bright sun is setting in the west,

its light lingers on my clothes.

The wind blows round and round the walls,

birds huddle together against the cold.

The Zhouzhou bird needs a mate to hold him when he dips and drinks,

the Qiongqiong beast needs another to help him feed.

But those men in power! O!

they forget their way out of the labyrinth!

How could I strive for vainglorious fame,

weakening my body, depressing my heart?

I'd rather flutter with the sparrow

than soar with the swan:

the swan may traverse the ocean,

but which is my way home, once I fly out from its heart?

九

步出上东门,
北望首阳岑。
下有采薇士,
上有嘉树林。
良辰在何许,
凝霜沾衣襟。
寒风振山冈,
玄云起重阴。
鸣雁飞南征,
鹍鸡发哀音。
素质游商声,
悽怆伤我心。

9

I pass through the Eastern Gate,

and look northwards, towards Shouyang Mountain:

at its foot, there are recluses picking and eating ferns,[1]

at its peak, there are beautiful forests.

When will we see the hour of brightness?

Frost condenses and wets my clothes.

Wind shocks the hills,

Clouds thicken in the dark sky.

I hear the geese, southwards, crying,

and the cuckoo's sorrowful song.

An Autumn note wafts in the frosty scene,

it is desolate, and saddens my heart.

---

1 商朝被灭后，伯夷和叔齐出于对商朝的忠心，逃到首阳山，采食薇草，最终饿死。他们的事迹见于司马迁（公元前 145—前 86）的《史记》中的《伯夷列传》。阮籍在《咏怀诗》多次用此典故。
After the Shang dynasty was overthrown, Boyi and Shuqi, out of loyalty to the Shang, fled to the Shouyang Mountain. There they collected ferns to eat and eventually died of hunger. See the "Biography of Boyi" in the *Records of the Grand Historian* by Sima Qian (145–86 BCE). Ruan Ji often used this allusion in *Songs of My Heart*.

十一

湛湛长江水,
上有枫树林。
皋兰被径路,
青骊逝骎骎。
远望令人悲,
春气感我心。

11

Deeply the Yangtze River flows

through thick forest of maple.

The marsh paths are strewn with violets[1],

and a black horse is galloping onwards.

Gazing into the distance makes me sad,

the Spring air moves my heart.

---

1 众所周知,《楚辞》奠定了中国诗歌中"香草美人"的传统,此后"兰"便成为美丽与纯洁的象征。在效果上,英诗中与之对应的是 violet。在汉诗英译中,人们通常使用 orchid 来翻译"兰",但 orchid 在传统英诗当中很少使用。如今在西方汉学界,有人主张用 thoroughwort、eupatorium 来翻译"兰"。虽然这些词表述了与"兰"对应的实际植物,但由于它们缺乏诗意联想,而且在一般语言交流中极少使用,因此无法产生与"兰"相应的诗意效果。为此,我们在翻译"兰"时,使用了 violet,因为我们所要翻译的,乃是诗意效果,而不是科学数据。"兰"作为形容词,又有优雅美好的宽泛意义,我们在翻译它时,也做了适当调整。As is well known, the *Songs of Chu* established the "fragrant plant and fair one" convention in Chinese poetry; thereafter, *lan* became a symbol of beauty and purity. In poetic effect, its English equivalent is "violet." In translating *lan*, many translators use "orchid", which is seldomly used in traditional English poetry. Nowadays in sinological research, some scholars advocate using "thoroughwort" or "eupatorium" to translate *lan*. Although these words convey a scientific and factual equivalent to *lan*, they evoke no similar poetic effect in English readers; in fact they are rarely used in common parlance at all. For this reason, we have adopted "violet" in our rendering of *lan*, because we aim to translate poetic effect, not scientific fact. *Lan* is also used as an adjective, describing something that is beautiful and elegant; in our rendering of this meaning we have also made some adjustments.

三楚多秀士，
朝云进荒淫。
朱华振芬芳，
高蔡相追寻。
一为黄雀哀，
涕下谁能禁？

The land of Chu used to teem with fine scholars

who wrote licentious tales to amuse their king.

They were like red, fragrant flowers,

pursuing each other to seek indulgence.

Once there was a yellow sparrow

      who thought that it had no predators –

thinking of him, who can hold back my tears?

十三

登高临四野,
北望青山阿。
松柏翳冈岑,
飞鸟鸣相过。
感慨怀辛酸,
怨毒常苦多。
李公悲东门,
苏子狭三河。
求仁自得仁,
岂复叹咨嗟!

13

I climbed high, and looked out across the wilderness.

To the north, the mountains, shadowed with green pines,

birds flying by, alone, crying.

The sorrow returns.

My life has been full of anguish.

I thought of Gentleman Li, in jail,

    who pined for the freedom at Eastern Gate.[1]

And Su[2], for whom the whole of Three Rivers

    was still too small a place.

And me? I sought only virtue,

and lo, I have been rewarded with virtue.

Why should I complain?

---

1 李斯为秦朝（公元前259—前210）丞相，被秦二世所杀。临刑前曾对其子说："我要和你一起牵着黄犬从上蔡的东门出去，可能吗？" Gentleman Li (Li Si) was the prime minister of the Qin dynasty (259-210 BCE). Before he was executed by the second emperor of the Qin, he said to his son: "I would like to take the yellow dog with you and take a walk out of the Eastern Gate at Shangcai, but how was that possible?"

2 苏子指的是战国（公元前403—前221）期间著名的说客苏秦。Su refers to Su Qin, a famous rhetorician during the Warring States period (403-221 BCE).

十四

开秋肇凉气,
蟋蟀鸣床帷。
感物怀殷忧,
悄悄令心悲。
多言焉所告,
繁辞将诉谁?
微风吹罗袂,
明月耀清晖。
晨鸡鸣高树,
命驾起旋归。

14

Autumn: I know that it's going to be cold;

lying in bed, listening to the cricket sing

the other side of the curtain, I am fearful,

saddened by this little natural thing.

A swelling heart, with whom to share?

A sea of words, with whom to speak?

Gently the breeze tugs at my silken sleeves.

The moon is bright, it shines like ice.

I hear the cockerel crow in the tree-top

and order my horse to be saddled. Time to return.

十五

昔年十四五,
志尚好书诗。
被褐怀珠玉,
颜闵相与期。
开轩临四野,
登高望所思。
丘墓蔽山冈,
万代同一时。
千秋万岁后,
荣名安所之?
乃悟羡门子,
嗷嗷令自嗤。

15

Years ago, at fourteen and fifteen,

I set my mind high on poetry and books.

Wearing coarse clothes, I cherished the ruby and pearl,

setting Yan Yuan and Min Sun[1] up as my models.

In an open cart I turned my face to the wide fields,

climbing ever upward I sought to follow my heroes.

The mounds of graves cover the hillsides,

thousands of years have passed in a single moment,

thousands of Autumns, tens of thousands of years –

what place can fame and glory hold?

Now I know the truth of the gods,

and laugh at myself, my rolling tears.

---

1 颜、闵指颜渊和闵损，二人系孔子的得意门生。Yan Yuan and Min Sun are two favorite students of Confucius.

十六

徘徊蓬池上,
还顾望大梁。
绿水扬洪波,
旷野莽茫茫。
走兽交横驰,
飞鸟相随翔。
是时鹑火中,
日月正相望。
朔风厉严寒,
阴气下微霜。
羁旅无俦匹,
俯仰怀哀伤。
小人计其功,
君子道其常。
岂惜终憔悴,
咏言著斯章。

16

Walking back and forth by Peng Lake,

my eyes settle on Daliang:

big waves flow ceaselessly down the blue water,

the vast wilderness stretches far away,

where animals' tracks run back and forth

and birds are flying, each with another.

The time is between September and October –

the Sun and the Moon stare into each other's eyes

and the wind blows fiercely from the north

crystallizing the damp air into thin frost.

I am a stranger here, a loner,

each nod of the head brings sadness.

Petty men there are, seeking personal gain,

and gentlemen, acting as gentlemen will.

Thin and pale as a ghost, I have no regret,

mumbling and chanting I write this poem.

十七

独坐空堂上,
谁可与欢者?
出门临永路,
不见行车马。
登高望九州,
悠悠分旷野。
孤鸟西北飞,
离兽东南下。
日暮思亲友,
晤言用自写。

17

I sit along in the empty courtyard.

Where is the man to whom I can bare my heart?

Outside, before me, stretches the endless road,

an empty road – no cart, no horses.

Climbing, I look over the Nine States[1] –

vast, so vast, they stretch before me.

One bird only, heading northwest,

and some little animal, lost, scurrying the other way.

Evening's the time when I miss my friends the most;

to comfort me, I write of our conversation.

---

1 九州指中国。The Nine States refers to China.

十九

西方有佳人,
皎若白日光,
被服纤罗衣,
左右佩双璜。
修容耀姿美,
顺风振微芳。
登高眺所思,
举袂当朝阳。
寄颜云霄间,
挥袖凌虚翔。
飘飖恍惚中,
流眄顾我旁。
悦怿未交接,
晤言用感伤。

19

There is a fair woman in the west

who is as bright as sunlight.

She wears a dress of the finest silk,

jewelry shines from her left, her right.

Her face is a charm, so full of grace,

lightly perfuming the breeze.

Climbing upward, she keeps watch for her loved one,

holding her sleeves, she faces the morning sun.

She hovers, she drifts through the sky,

waving her sleeves, she dances in the void,

flies like the wind, like a cloud, in trance.

Every so often, she glances at me,

but for me this beauty is out of reach.

Left alone, I lament my fate.

二十

杨朱泣歧路,
墨子悲染丝。
揖让长离别,
飘飖难与期。
岂徒燕婉情,
存亡诚有之。
萧索人所悲,
祸衅不可辞。
赵女媚中山,
谦柔愈见欺。
嗟嗟途上士,
何用自保持?

20

Yang Zhu wept for the sheer number of crossroads,
Mozi grieved that the white silk could be dyed into different colors.[1]
We held our hands to bid each other a long farewell,
when could we expect to meet again in this turbulent world?
This was not mere sentimentality, un-called for,
but a matter of life and death.
We lament the sufferings of this world,
misfortune and disaster cannot be avoided.
The fair girl of Zhao deceived the King of Dai,
modesty and tenderness only make one more exposed.
O! I think of the common scholars, treading along their roads,
Where can they find their peace and safety?

1　杨朱、墨子均为战国时期的思想家。Yang Zhu and Mozi are thinkers during the Warring States period.

二十一

于心怀寸阴,
羲阳将欲冥。
挥袂抚长剑,
仰观浮云征。
云间有玄鹤,
抗志扬哀声。
一飞冲青天,
旷世不再鸣。
岂与鹑鷃游,
连翩戏中庭。

21

In my heart I treasure every moment of time,

the sun will soon descend into darkness.

Waving my sleeves I brandish the long sword

and holding my head aloft, I watch the clouds in their courses.

Among them I see a black crane,

firm in its will, making its sad sounds.

Once it darts away, into the blue sky,

its cry will be gone forever.

How can he flutter and flap around with the quails

playing down there in the courtyard?

二十三

东南有射山，
汾水出其阳。
六龙服气舆，
云盖切天纲。
仙者四五人，
逍遥晏兰房。
寝息一纯和，
呼噏成露霜。
沐浴丹渊中，
照耀日月光。
岂安通灵台，
游濛去高翔。

23

In the southeast the holy Guye Mountain rises,

from its southern side the Fen River flows.

Six dragons drive the airy chariot,

the cloud canopy approaches the Star of Tiangang.

Four or five celestial beings

rest at leisure in the graceful house –

in sleep, their breathing is pure and harmonious,

at dawn their breath becomes dew and frost.

They bathe in the deep cinnabar pool

on which the sun and bright moon shines.

Easy and carefree of heart and soul,

upward they soar, to heaven.

二十四

殷忧令志结，
怵惕常若惊。
逍遥未终晏，
朱华忽西倾。
蟋蟀在户牖，
蟪蛄号中庭。
心肠未相好，
谁云亮我情？
愿为云间鸟，
千里一哀鸣。
三芝延瀛洲，
远游可长生。

24

Deep depression makes a knot of heart.
To be always on edge is a permanent state of shock.
Before your pleasure has reached its height
the sun sets, suddenly red in the west.
Crickets are chirruping under the window,
Huigu, the short-lived cicada, down in the courtyard.
The hearts of men are estranged from each other.
Who understands, or believes, my feelings?
I wish I could be a bird in the clouds
whose melancholy song is heard through a thousand *li*.
The elixir plant Sanzhi covers the slope of Yingzhou,
I'll travel there to live forever.

二十五

拔剑临白刃,
安能相中伤。
但畏工言子,
称我三江旁。
飞泉流玉山,
悬车栖扶桑。
日月径千里,
素风发微霜。
势路有穷达,
咨嗟安可长。

25

I would rather face the edge of a drawn sword
than serve in this slanderous court.
The only thing that frightens me is sophistication –
men who try to trap me with their insidious talk.
The flying fountain hangs in the Mountain of Jade,
the sun's chariot stands at rest in the east.
The sun and the moon travel a thousand *li* each day,
the Autumn wind brings a thin frost.
Yes, the road of official career roams up and down,
no need to sigh for long.

二十六

朝登洪坡颠,
日夕望西山。
荆棘被原野,
群鸟飞翩翩。
鸾鹥时栖宿,
性命有自然。
建木谁能近?
射干复婵娟。
不见林中葛,
延蔓相勾连?

26

In the morning, I climbed to the hilltop,

at sunset, I kept my eyes on the West Mountain.

Thorns covered the open fields,

flocks of graceful birds flew by.

Phoenixes perch with their own kind,

all of life follows its natural course.

Who can come close to the magical Jianmu tree?

The Yegan flower displays its elegance by the cliff.

Don't you see the vines in the forest,

twined together, all the way from the root?

二十八

若木耀西海,
扶桑翳瀛洲。
日月经天涂,
明暗不相雠。
穷达自有常,
得失又何求?
岂效路上童,
携手共遨游?
阴阳有变化,
谁云沉不浮?
朱鳖跃飞泉,
夜飞过吴洲。
俯仰运天地,
再俯四海流。
系累名利场,
驽骏同一辀,
岂若遗耳目,
升遐去殷忧?

28

Ruomu[1] illuminates the Western Sea,
Fusang[2] casts its shadow on Yingzhou Peak[3].
The sun and the moon cross the sky on their own roads,
light and darkness never travel together.
Poverty and prosperity also have their ways,
loss and gain cannot be made by force.
How can I imitate those children, there on road
who run and play with their arms entwined?
Yin and Yang change over, as is their wont,
who says that if you sink you can never resurface?
The red river-turtle jumps across the flying fountain,
King Wu's sword flies over the land of Wu.
Sinking, rising, I move with the course of nature,
and rest with the flow of the Four Seas.
Burdened with fame and wealth,
the nag and steed are tied to the self-same cart.
Why not clear my eyes and ears of all this
and fly far away, deserting dejection?

---

1 若木生于西方昆仑山。The Ruomu tree grows on the Kunlun Mountain in the west.
2 扶桑为日出之处。The Fusang tree is where the sun rises.
3 瀛洲为渤海中仙山。Yingzhou is a magical mountain in the Bohai Sea.

三十

驱车出门去,
意欲远征行。
征行安所如?
背弃夸与名。
夸名不在己,
但愿适中情。
单帷蔽皎日,
高榭隔微声。
谗邪使交疏,
浮云令昼冥。
嬿婉同衣裳,
一顾倾人城。
从容在一时,
繁花不再荣。
晨朝奄复暮,
不见所欢形。
黄鸟东南飞,
寄言谢友生。

I clambered aboard my cart and left,
wishing to embark on a long journey.
What was the goal of my journey?
The abandonment of vanity and fame.
Vanity and fame do not rely on will –
best to follow your innermost heart.
A single curtain can cut off the sunlight,
the high pavilion muffles the slightest tones.
Calumny separates intimate friends,
floating clouds darken the bright sky.
Look at that fair, alluring woman, sharing clothes with others,
a single glance from her topples a whole state.
Fortune, success, come for a moment and go,
flowers, once bloomed, will never blossom again.
Quickly morning passes to become evening,
the shape of my beloved is nowhere to be seen.
O yellow bird! Fly southeast
and carry these words to my friend.

三十二

朝阳不再盛,
白日忽西幽。
去此若俯仰,
如何似九秋?
人生若尘露,
天道邈悠悠。
齐景升丘山,
涕泗纷交流。
孔圣临长川,
惜逝忽若浮。
去者余不及,
来者吾不留。
愿登太华山,
上与松子游。
渔父知世患,
乘流泛轻舟。

32

The morning sun will never be as bright again,

and the day grows suddenly dark in the west.

This parting is only a brief moment, a nod of head,

who says it endures Autumn long?

The life of Man is like the dew on the dust.

How long, and how vast, is the Way of Heaven!

The Duke of Qi looked down from the hill –

tears fell down his face like streams crossing.

Sage Confucius stood by the long river,

lamenting time, so swiftly flowing.

What is past I cannot regain,

and what's to come I cannot keep.

I wish that I could climb the Taihua Mountain

and live up there in heaven, among the gods!

The fisherman knew the sufferings of this world,

so, taking a little skiff, he drifted along with the current.

三十三

一日复一夕,
一夕复一朝。
颜色改平常,
精神自损消。
胸中怀汤火,
变化故相招。
万事无穷极,
智谋苦不饶,
但恐须臾间,
魂气随风飘。
终身履薄冰,
谁知我心焦?

33

Days after evenings

evenings after mornings

the countenances loses its color

the spirit weakens of itself.

A fire is raging within my chest –

everything changes thereby, one thing after another.

Universal phenomena have no end

that Man's pitiful wit can ever penetrate.

My only fear is that in a moment's time

my soul will catch the wind and fly away.

All my life I've been walking on thin ice.

Who could know my anxious heart?

三十五

世务何缤纷,
人道苦不遑。
壮年以时逝,
朝露待太阳。
愿揽羲和辔,
白日不移光。
天阶路殊绝,
云汉邈无梁。
濯发旸谷滨,
远游昆岳傍。
登彼列仙岨,
采此秋兰芳。
时路乌足争,
太极可翱翔。

35

Worldly affairs are completely disordered,
and it's a pity that we can't stay long –
youth passes within an hour,
the morning dew awaits the sun.
I wish that I held the sun-cart's reign,
then its brilliant light would never pass!
The stairway to Heaven's a difficult climb,
and there is no bridge to cross the Milky Way.
Washing my hair by the side of the Yanggu River,
traveling far to Kunlun Peak –
there I climb the godly hills
to gather the fragrant Autumn violets.
The ways of the world are hardly worth competing for,
the vast Cosmos is the place to soar!

三十六

谁言万事艰,
逍遥可终生。
临堂翳华树,
悠悠念无形。
彷徨思亲友,
倏忽复至冥。
寄言东飞鸟,
可用慰我情。

36

Who says that life is hard?

Life can disappear in leisure:

in front of my courtyard there stands a feathery, flowery tree –

standing in its shade, I consider the formless cosmos...

Walking up and down I miss my relatives and friends,

and then the day is suddenly dark again.

Let those eastward-flying birds carry my message

and comfort my heart.

三十七

嘉时在今辰,
零雨洒尘埃。
临路望所思,
日夕复不来。
人情有感慨,
荡漾焉能排?
挥涕怀哀伤,
辛酸谁语哉?

37

This morning's hour of joy has come,

yet the drizzle moistens the dust.

I wait by the roadside for my beloved

until evening, still she doesn't come.

Human nature teems with sentiments –

they disturb me, how can I console myself?

With sadness in my heart I wipe away the tears.

Who will listen to these miserable words?

三十九

壮士何慷慨,
志欲威八荒。
驱车远行役,
受命念自忘。
良弓挟乌号,
明甲有精光。
临难不顾生,
身死魂飞扬。
岂为全躯士,
效命争疆场。
忠为百世荣,
义使令名彰。
垂声谢后世,
气节故有常。

39

How brave and how daring are those heroes!
Their only will is to strike the entire world.
Driving chariots to the far battlefield,
they cherish their leader's trust, forget their own safety.
They hold their wonderful bows in their hands,
their armor sheds a magnificent glint.
Confronting danger, they care little for their lives –
when they die, their souls spread out in the sky.
These are not cowards, only concerned with saving themselves,
they give themselves devotedly to battle.
Their loyalty will be glory for hundreds of generations,
their deeds will make their names well-known,
their fame will be honored by the world eternally,
their spiritual integrity will never suffer change.

四十一

天网弥四野,
六翮掩不舒。
随波纷纶客,
泛泛若浮凫。
生命无期度,
朝夕有不虞。
列仙停修龄,
养志在冲虚。
飘飖云日间,
邈与世路殊。
荣名非己宝,
声色焉足娱!
采药无旋返,
神仙志不符。
逼此良可惑,
令我久踌躇。

41

The Heavenly Web covers the wilderness,
the swan folds up her powerful wings
and follows the tide
with thousands of common ducks.
The life of a man can never be predicted:
mornings and evenings, the unexpected.
The immortals apply themselves to prolonging life:
fostering their will in nothingness,
they hover between the clouds and sun
far, far away from the ways of the world.
Fame and glory are not what I treasure,
women and music can never entertain me.
Those who seek the elixir vitae never return.
Even the words of immortals cannot be trusted!
And, when I think of this,
I find myself transfixed...

四十二

王业须良辅,
建功俟英雄。
元凯康哉美,
多士颂声隆。
阴阳有舛错,
日月不常融。
天时有否泰,
人事多盈冲。
园绮遁南岳,
伯阳隐西戎。
保身念道真,
宠耀焉足崇!
人谁不善始,
鲜能克厥终。
休哉上世士,
万载垂清风。

Kings and emperors require good advisors,
and to achieve outstanding things, heroic men are needed.
How brilliant and handsome the scholars used to be,
and how they prospered, ringing the air in praise of their rulers.
Yin and Yang have their time of discord,
the sun and the moon are not bright all of the time.
Nature's course is now harmonious, now discordant,
human affairs are often out of control!
Yuan and Qi hid themselves away in the mountains,[1]
Laozi became a recluse in the far West.
The truth of Dao is to hold to one's integrity,
favor and glory are not worth striving for.
Most men are capable of making a good start,
but only few can see things through to the end.
Yes, the scholars of ancient days are beautiful –
names that will be remembered forever.

---

1 园与绮指东园公和绮里季，汉代的隐士。Yuan and Qi refer to Master Dongyuan and Qi Liji, two recluses during the Han dynasty.

四十三

鸿鹄相随飞,
随飞适荒裔。
双翮临长风,
须臾万里逝。
朝餐琅玕实,
夕宿丹山际。
抗身青云中,
网罗孰能制?
岂与乡曲士,
携手共言誓?

43

Together the swans fly

to the distant end of the world.

They spread their wings and soar,

crossing thousands of *li* at a glance.

At dawn, they breakfast on manna,

at nightfall they rest on the godly mountain.

They hover among clouds –

is there a web or snare that could hold them?

Hah! Why should I mix with those country squires,

putting their hands on each other's hands,

    swearing their pacts?

四十四

俦物终始殊,
修短各异方。
琅玕生高山,
芝英耀朱堂。
荧荧桃李花,
成蹊将夭伤。
焉敢希千术,
三春表微光。
自非凌风树,
憔悴乌有常!

44

Similar things grow apart as life proceeds –
long and short, their lots change.
The godly tree has its home in the high mountain,
the numinous mushroom shines in the red courtyard.
How brilliantly the plum and peach trees bloom!
But once a path is trod beneath them they suffer ruin.
How can they yearn for the long, wide road?
They can only display their faint luster in Spring.
And me?
    I'm not the evergreen pine, against wind and frost,
decay just comes and goes.

四十七

生命辰安在?
忧戚涕沾襟。
高鸟翔山冈,
燕雀栖下林。
青云蔽前庭,
素琴悽我心。
崇山有鸣鹤,
岂可相追寻?

47

Where can we find the moment of our life?

Tears of grief dampen my sleeves.

The eagle glides above the mountain,

the sparrow perches below in the bushes.

Dark clouds cover the courtyard,

the zither's music saddens my heart.

The crane flies, singing, across the peak,

how can we follow him?

四十八

鸣鸠嬉庭树,
焦明游浮云。
焉见孤翔鸟,
翩翩无匹群。
死生自然理,
消散何缤纷。

48

Turtledoves play on the courtyard tree,

a phoenix glides by on the clouds.

Look at that lonely bird in the sky,

flying, slowly, with no companion...

Life and death depend on the Law of Nature,

always recurring, fading, extinction...

五十

清露为凝霜,
华草成蒿莱。
谁云君子贤,
明达安可能?
乘云招松乔,
呼嗡永矣哉。

50

The fresh dew congeals into frost,

the beautiful plants become weeds.

Who can talk about noble virtues,

and how can wisdom and enlightenment endure?

Riding the clouds, I seek the Immortals,

breathing pure air with them,

    breathing,

        breathing,

            alas!

五十二

十日出旸谷,
弭节驰万里。
经天耀四海,
倏忽潜濛汜。
谁言焱炎久?
游没何行俟。
逝者岂长生,
亦去荆与杞。
千岁犹崇朝,
一餐聊自已。
是非得失间,
焉足相讥理!
计利知术穷,
哀情遽能止。

52

The Ten Suns rise in the East,[1]

their drivers whip them onward, thousands of *li*.

Crossing the sky, they shine down upon the Four Seas,

suddenly, they sink in the West.

Who says their luster endures?

They stop and go forth in their long journey.

Those who are gone – who says their life was long?

They all have come to the place of thorns and thistles.

Thousands of years are just one morning.

Life disappears over a dinner-party.

Right and wrong, gain and loss –

how can it be worthwhile to vex oneself!

When schemes for profit come to an end,

so will the sadness of Man.

---

1 古代神话有十日并出的传说. In ancient mythology it was said that there were at one time ten suns in the sky.

五十三

自然有成理,
生死道无常。
智巧万端出,
大要不易方。
如何夸毗子,
作色怀骄肠。
乘轩驱良马,
凭几向膏粱。
被服纤罗衣,
深榭设闲房。
不见日夕华,
翩翩飞路旁。

53

Nature has its way of doing things,

the course of life and death can never be known.

From wisdom and tact evil and trouble come,

the Way of Universe never changes.

Look at those ignoble sycophants,

why are they strutting so arrogantly?

They ride in carriages pulled by the finest steeds,

sit at tables covered with the finest foods;

their clothes are cut from satin and silk,

and their chambers are hidden, deep, deep in the terraces –

Don't they see the flowers that bloom in daylight

are falling, at sunset, one by one, along the roadside?

五十四

夸谈快愤懑,
情慵发烦心。
西北登不周,
东南望邓林。
旷野弥九州,
崇山抗高岑。
一餐度万世,
千岁再浮沉。
谁云玉石同?
泪下不可禁。

54

Boastful talks relieve one's anger,

but laziness only breeds anxiety.

So, heading Northwest, I climb up Buzhou Mountain,

and turn Southeast to stare at the Forest of Deng.

A great expanse of wilderness, stretching across the land,

the hills are lifted up on the backs of enormous mountains.

An age is spent in the time it takes to eat,

thousands of years, just a rise and fall.

Who says that jade and rock are of the self-same kind?

Nothing to do to restrain these tears.

五十五

人言愿延年,
延年欲焉之?
黄鹄呼子安,
千秋未可期。
独坐山岩中,
恻怆怀所思。
王子一何好,
猗靡相携持。
悦怿犹今辰,
计较在一时。
置此明朝事,
日夕将见欺。

55

People say they wish to prolong their lives.

Having done that, where can they go from there?

The yellow crane calls out to its immortal rider –

such a fate can never be expected.

Alone, I sit among the mountain rocks,

my heart is sore, and misses my beloved.

Prince Jin, that god, is truly beautiful!

I wish I could grow intimate with him.

Love and harmony can only be found today;

now is the only moment for our planning.

Give up any thoughts about tomorrow,

this very evening we will find ourselves deceived.

五十七

惊风振四野,
回云荫堂隅。
床帷为谁设?
几杖为谁扶?
虽非明君子,
岂闇桑与榆!
世有此聋瞆,
芒芒将焉如?
翩翩从风飞,
悠悠去故居。
离麾玉山下,
遗弃毁与誉。

57

The tempest strikes the wild earth,

flying clouds darken the courtyard.

For whom is the bed-curtain hung?

For whom am I leaning on the stick and table?

Though I'm not gifted myself with uncanny sight,

still my vision is not dim as I grow old:

the world is filled with the deaf and the dumb,

where can I go in this vast country?

I want to fly with a light heart, in the wind,

far, far away from this my native land,

until I arrive at the Jade Mountain,

leaving abandoned all slander and praise.

五十八

危冠切浮云,
长剑出天外。
细故何足虑,
高度跨一世。
非子为我御,
逍遥游荒裔。
顾谢西王母,
吾将从此逝。
岂与蓬户士,
弹琴诵言誓?

My high hat divides the floating clouds,

my sword stretches out to the end of the sky.

The trifles of this world are no concern of mine,

I stand on high to overlook all this.

With Feizi as my driver I will gallop away,[1]

and wander in the wilderness with an easy heart.

I bid farewell to the Queen Mother of the West.[2]

The goal of my journey is still to be reached.

How could I mix with those poor, narrow-minded scholars,

chanting their books, playing their harps, and swearing their oaths?

---

1 《史记·秦本纪》中记载了一位善于养马、名叫非子的人。In the "Chronicles of the Qin Dynasty" chapter of the *Records of the Grand Historian*, there was a good horse-breeder named Feizi.
2 西王母为古代神话中的仙人。The Queen Mother of the West is a deity in ancient mythology.

六十

儒者通六艺,
立志不可干。
违礼不为动,
非法不肯言。
渴饮清泉流,
饥食并一箪。
岁时无以祀,
衣服常苦寒。
屣履咏南风,
缊袍笑华轩。
信道守诗书,
义不受一餐。
烈烈褒贬词,
老氏用长叹。

60

The Confucianists are well-versed in the Six Classics,
no one can shake their tenacious will.

They never act in discord with the rituals,
they'll never speak against the rules.

Thirsty, they drink from clear fountains,
hungry, they eat from bamboo bowls every two days.

When times of sacrifice come, they can offer nothing,
their shabby clothes can barely protect them against the cold.

But on they trudge, chanting songs of an ancient sage,
mocking in their tatters the carriage of the rich.

Loyal to their beliefs they live among books,
refusing handouts for justice's sake.

For this, they are both praised and vilified –
Laozi, however, merely exhaled his sighs.

六十二

平昼整衣冠,
思见客与宾。
宾客者谁子?
倏忽若飞尘。
裳衣佩云气,
言语究灵神。
须臾相背弃,
何时见斯人?

62

Dressing up at noon,

I long to meet a guest.

Who is this guest?

He is as uncertain as the flying dust,

clouds and air are his clothes,

gods and spirits his topic.

He abandons me at a glance.

When can I meet this character?

六十四

朝出上东门,
遥望首阳基。
松柏郁森沉,
鹂黄相与嬉。
逍遥九曲间,
徘徊欲何之?
念我平居时,
郁然思妖姬。

64

When morning came, I walked out from the Eastern Gate
and gazed across at Shouyang Mountain in the distance.[1]
Dense pines cast deep shadows across its face,
and orioles played, one with another.
Strolling among the meandering streams,
haltingly, unsure of my direction,
all the routine of my everyday life came into my mind.
My deep thought turned to that beautiful woman...

---

[1] 首阳山为古代隐士伯夷和叔齐隐居之处。The Shouyang Mountain is where the ancient recluses Boyi and Shuqi escaped to.

六十五

王子十五年,
游衍伊洛滨。
朱颜茂春华,
辩慧怀清真。
焉见浮丘公,
举手谢时人。
轻荡易恍惚,
飘飖弃其身。
飞飞鸣且翔,
挥翼且酸辛。

This prince was fifteen years of age
when he traveled along the Yi and Luo Rivers.[1]
His face was blooming and red as a Spring flower,
his wit was quick and his heart innocent.
Then he met up with Master Fuqiu,
and bade farewell to everyone here for good.
Lost in trance, forsaking his body,
he drifted away on the wind,
hovering, singing,
    and feeling a little sore,
        with outstretched wings.

---

1 此诗用的是《列仙传》中王子乔（又称王子晋）于伊洛水间遇道士浮丘公，因而成仙的故事。This poem alludes to a story from *Biographies of Immortals*. Prince Qiao, also known as Prince Jin, chanced to meet Master Fuqiu, a Daoist monk, along the Yi and Luo Rivers; the two subsequently became immortals.

六十七

洪生资制度,
被服正有常。
尊卑设次序,
事物齐纪纲。
容饰整颜色,
磬折执圭璋。
堂上置玄酒,
室中盛稻粱。
外厉贞素谈,
户内灭芬芳。
放口从衷出,
复说道义方。
委曲周旋仪,
姿态愁我肠。

67

The renown of Confucian scholars relies on certain rules:
they dress according to convention,
a definite line is drawn between the superior and inferior,
and every thing, and every act, is strictly set.
Every facial gesture, every stroke of makeup,
every piece of jade worn at court is designed to impress.
In their courtyard the ceremonial water is stored,
and the ritual rice in their houses.
In public they put on solemn and noble airs,
at home all beautiful things are extinguished.
Occasionally they let go of some heartfelt words,
but resume moral rhetoric before a minute passes.
How affected and pretentious are their manners!
They depress me.

六十九

人知结交易,
交友诚独难。
险路多疑惑,
明珠未可干。
彼求飨太牢,
我欲并一餐。
损益生怨毒,
咄咄复何言!

69

All of us know how easy it is to associate with others,

but to make true friends is indeed a difficult thing.

The path of life is dangerous, people grow suspicious,

the ruby glows beyond our reach.

That man wants to eat the food of kings,

but for me, a meal in two days is enough.

Reducing his share and adding to mine will anger us both,

and any debate on this is just a waste of breath.

七十

有悲则有情,
无悲亦无思。
苟非婴网罟,
何必万里畿?
翔风拂重霄,
庆云招所晞。
灰心寄枯宅,
曷顾人间姿?
始得忘我难,
焉知嘿自遗。

70

The man of sorrow is a man of sensibility,

but without sorrow there is no consideration.

If traps and snares were not awaiting me,

why should I need to travel so far and wide?

Floating on the wind, I touch the depth of the sky.

The rainbow clouds dance brilliantly in sunlight.

Heart like ashes, residing in a body like a withered tree,

why should I bother about the affairs of men?

One can understand the difficulty of self-forgetting,

if he knows that in silence he can leave himself behind.

七十一

木槿荣丘墓,
煌煌有光色。
白日颓林中,
翩翩零路侧。
蟋蟀吟户牖,
蟪蛄鸣荆棘。
蜉蝣玩三朝,
采采修羽翼。
衣裳为谁施?
俛仰自收拭。
生命几何时,
慷慨各努力。

71

The rose mallows blossom on the rolling graves,

they are lovely, and luminous.

The radiant sun goes down into the trees

as one by one, the flowers fall by the road.

Outside my window a cricket is singing,

the short-lived cicada moans in the thorn.

Mayflies play for their three days' life,

together they polish their bright wings.

For whom they are wearing their costumes?

To perfect their little moment.

The life of Man is also brief.

Our hearts know it. We should
                        try our best to live.

七十二

修涂驰轩车,
长川载轻舟。
性命岂自然,
势路有所由。
高名令志惑,
重利使心忧。
亲昵怀反侧,
骨肉还相雠。
更希毁珠玉,
可用登遨游。

72

The long trail is appropriate for the carriage,

the river, wide and long, bears up the light boat.

How can human life be determined by nature's course

when fame and wealth so affect our desires?

This longing for fame confuses the will,

and for riches, worries the heart.

Friends act inconsistently towards one another

and people of self-same blood become each other's foes.

I wish to do away with all the pearls and rubies in the world,

then I could roam and climb, easy and buoyant-hearted.

七十四

猗欤上世士,
恬淡志安贫。
季叶道陵迟,
驰骛纷垢尘。
宁子岂不类?
杨歌谁肯殉?
栖栖非我偶,
徨徨非己伦。
咄嗟荣辱事,
去来味道真。

O, the scholars of bygone days,

indifferent to ambition, living the simple life!

In this degenerate world, the Way declines –

people rush here and there, everywhere dirt and dust.

How can we say that Ning Qi[1] is ignoble?

Who can be enlightened by Yang Zhu's song on death?[2]

Restless people are not my companions,

those who bustle and rush are not my type.

Glory and shame can change in a breath,

the Way comes and goes, revealing to me its truth.

---

1 宁子指宁戚，战国时期人。他起初因贫困无法得到齐国国王的赏识，后被委以要职。Ning Qi lived in the Qi state during the Warring States period. At first he was unable to gain recognition of the King because of his poverty. Later he was given an important post in the government.

2 杨朱之友季梁病重，其子在身边哭泣，并为之请医。季梁请杨朱用歌来开导他们。杨朱因而吟唱生死乃"天其弗识，人胡能觉"的自然现象，但季梁之子终未晓悟，继续为其父请医。此事见《列子》。According to *Liezi*, Yang Zhu's friend Ji Liang was gravely ill, and his sons wept by him and sent for a doctor. Ji Liang asked Yang Zhu to sing a song to enlighten his sons. Yang Zhu sang that life and death were natural courses, which even "Heaven cannot understand,/ How can man fathom?" But Ji Liang's sons persisted in asking help from a doctor.

道真信可娱,
清洁存精神。
巢由抗高节,
从此适河滨。

The Way's truth is indeed a pleasant thing –
in innocence and purity the spirit is retained.
Chaofu and Xu You[1] are both noble characters,
from now on, I too will go down to the riverside.

1 巢父、许由均为上古著名的隐士。Chaofu and Xu You were famous hermits of antiquity.

七十五

梁东有芳草,
一朝再三荣。
色容艳姿美,
光华耀倾城。
岂为明哲士,
妖蛊诒媚生。
轻薄在一时,
安知百世名?
路端便娟子,
但恐日月倾。
焉见冥灵木?
悠悠竟无形。

75

At Liangdong, fragrant flowers grow

which blossom many times in a single day.

Lovely their faces, gestures, charming,

shining through the town.

But how can one be wise enough to protect himself,

when seduction and flattery rise up everywhere?

Dandyism and frivolity are gone in a moment,

how can they know the name that endures forever?

Fair ones! at the end of the road,

fearful of sunset, moonset,

can't you see the magical Mingling tree?

It loses its shape in the vastness of space.

七十六

秋驾安可学?
东野穷路旁。
纶深鱼渊潜,
矰设鸟高翔。
泛泛乘轻舟,
演漾靡所望。
吹嘘谁以益?
江湖相捐忘。
都冶难为颜,
修容是我常。
兹年在松乔,
恍惚诚未央。

How can you learn to ride as fast as flying?

Dongye lost his over-used horses by the road.

Fish swim in the deep water below the hook,

birds fly high above the trap –

I will take a little boat, and float downstream

to where there is nothing to see but endless water.

What good is it, to moisten each other after we are beached?

Better forgetting each other in water or lake.[1]

It's a difficult thing to be fair of face –

just to keep myself clean is enough for me.

Longevity belongs to the gods and goddesses,

living in endless trance.

---

1 《庄子·大宗师》讲到河水干涸后，鱼搁浅在陆地上，彼此用嘴互相吹润，以期存活。在庄子看来，与其如此，不如它们在江湖中彼此相忘。"The Great Master" chapter of *Zhuangzi* notes that when the lake dries up, the beached fish moisten each other with their mouths in order to survive. It would be much better, Zhuangzi stated, that they forget each other in the river or lake.

七十七

咄嗟行至老,
俛偲常苦忧。
临川羡洪波,
同始异支流。
百年何足言?
但苦怨与雠。
雠怨者谁子?
耳目还相羞。
声色为胡越,
人情自逼遒。
招彼玄通士,
去来归羡游。

77

In a moment of breath old age arrives,

yet always worry, always anxiety.

I stand by the rivers, envying their ceaseless motion,

out from a single source dividing.

A hundred years is hardly worth talking about!

Hatred and resentment harass me.

Who are these people, hating and resenting?

Even the eyes and ears scorn one another,

sound and color – distinct as North and South!

Human feelings persecute each other.

How I long to meet that scholar, well-versed in mystery,

that we may come and go, strolling along the course of nature.

七十八

昔有神仙士,
乃处射山阿。
乘云御飞龙,
嘘噏叽琼华。
可闻不可见,
慷慨叹咨嗟。
自伤非俦类,
愁苦来相加。
下学而上达,
忽忽将如何?

Once upon a time there was a god

who lived on the Guye Mountain.

Riding dragons, flying on clouds,

he breathed immortal air, he ate ambrosia.

He could be heard, but he couldn't be seen –

Oh how I am moved by this!

I lament my fate for not being one of his caste,

distress and anxiety add to my state.

"I study below, but my learning penetrates Heaven." [1]

Suddenly, the times have changed.

    Where should I head for now?

---

[1] 孔子曾说:"下学而上达,知我者其天乎。" Confucius once said, "I study below, but my learning penetrates Heaven. Only Heaven knows me."

Ruan Ji

七十九

林中有奇鸟,
自言是凤凰。
清朝饮醴泉,
日夕栖山冈。
高鸣彻九州,
延颈望八荒。
适逢商风起,
羽翼自摧藏。
一去昆仑西,
何时复回翔?
但恨处非位,
怆恨使心伤。

In the forest there dwells an extraordinary bird

who calls himself a phoenix.

Mornings he drinks from the sweet fountain,

evenings he rests on the mountain top.

His sonorous singing penetrates the entire land,

he stretches his neck and peers across the wilderness.

When the Autumn winds begin to blow

and cracks his wings,

he flies to the western side of Kunlun Mountain.

No one knows the time of his return.

I regret being not like him

and such a regret wounds my heart.

八十

出门望佳人,
佳人岂在兹?
三山招松乔,
万世谁与期?
存亡有长短,
慷慨将焉知?
忽忽朝日隤,
行行将何之?
不见季秋草,
摧折在今时?

80

Walking through the gate I gazed around for my beloved.

Is my beloved here?

The godly Three Mountains attract the immortals,

who amongst us can expect to accompany them?

Life and death are short and long –

Deeply moved, what I can know from this?

The morning sun sets suddenly –

moving, moving, which way should I take?

Don't you see those late Autumn plants?

Even now they are broken down and destroyed.

八十一

昔有神仙者,
羡门及松乔。
噏习九阳间,
升遐叽云霄。
人生乐长久,
百年自言辽。
白日陨隅谷,
一夕不再朝。
岂若遗世物,
登明随飘飖。

81

Once upon a time those immortals
called Xianmen, Chisong and Prince Qiao
lived in state at the edge of the sky.
They flew up to take clouds as their food.
Man yearns for a long life,
a hundred years is far, far away.
The bright sun sets in the valley,
evening never turns to morning.
So much better to leave all worldly things behind
and ascend to the sky to hover with the wind!

八十二

墓前荧荧者,
木槿耀朱华。
荣好未终朝,
连飙陨其葩。
岂若西山草,
琅玕与丹禾。
垂影临增城,
余光照九阿。
宁微少年子,
日夕叹咨嗟。

The rose mallows are blossoming,

and shining by the graves.

Their charm, their beauty, have not lasted one morning

before they're shattered by the ceaseless wind ...

How can they be like the magical Langgan and Danhe,

which grow like grass on the West Mountain?

They stand on the high cliffs and cast shadows,

their light lingers upon the vast slopes.

Surely some youngsters sigh

as the day draws to its end ...

嵇 康

Ji Kang

嵇康（224—263），字叔夜，魏晋时期另一名士，常与阮籍并称。他博闻多识，对音乐、养生均有研究，犹好老庄。他超然不群，蔑视礼法，提出"越名教而任自然"，因此曾冒犯权贵。竹林七贤另一成员、友人山涛举荐他出仕为官，嵇康断然拒绝，并写下千古传诵的《与山巨源绝交书》。其友吕安为人陷害，嵇康为之出庭作证，二人一同被害。时三千太学生为其请愿，请以为师，当权者不为所动。嵇康善于论理，所作论文条分缕析，为后世所传诵。

Ji Kang (224–263), courtesy name Shuye, was often named together with Ruan Ji as another outstanding literatus of the Wei-Jin era. A widely knowledgeable man, he showed deep interest and expertise in the art of music and alchemy, and was particularly passionate about the teachings of Laozi and Zhuangzi. He chose to live apart from the norms of society, and advocated to "transcend doctrines and follow nature," which alarmed and offended some powerful people in the court. His friend Shan Tao, who was another member of the Seven

Worthies of the Bamboo Grove, once recommended Ji Kang for a government position; Ji Kang flatly refused, and wrote the famed "Farewell to Shan Juyuan [Tao]," which became an instant classic. When his friend Lü An was slandered and charged in a defamation case, Ji Kang testified on his behalf. Seizing this opportunity, the authorities executed both of them. Before Ji Kang's execution, three thousand students from the Imperial Academy petitioned the government to appoint him as their teacher, but the government refused. Ji Kang was particularly known for his ability at rational reasoning and argument; his essays are all carefully, clearly thought out and forcefully presented; they have been greatly treasured throughout the Chinese tradition.

秋胡行七章

一

富贵尊荣,
忧患谅独多。
富贵尊荣,
忧患谅独多。
古人所惧,
丰屋蔀家。
人害其上,
兽恶网罗。
惟有贫贱,
可以无他。
歌以言之,
富贵忧患多。

A Qiu Hu Song (in seven stanzas)

1

Wealth, glory and power

bring suffering and anxiety.

Wealth, glory and power

bring suffering and anxiety.

What the ancients feared most

was owning too grand a dwelling.

People dread what comes from above,

as animals dread the trap.

Only a life of poverty

can free us from disaster.

I sing to make it clear:

Wealth and power bring about suffering.

二

贫贱易居,
贵盛难为工。
贫贱易居,
贵盛难为工。
耻接直言,
与祸相逢。
变故万端,
俾吉作凶。
思牵黄犬,
其计莫从。
歌以言之,
贵盛难为工。

2

One can get used to poverty,

but rank and wealth are harder to cope with.

One can get used to poverty,

but rank and wealth are harder to cope with.

If a man is too proud to take frank advice,

he will meet with misfortune.

The unexpected may come any moment,

our happy lives turned to calamity.

Li Si wanted to walk his yellow dog,

but his simple desire was thwarted.[1]

I sing to make it clear:

rank and wealth are hard to cope with.

---

[1] 据《史记·李斯列传》，秦朝宰相李斯在临刑之前，曾对其子说："吾欲与若复牵黄犬，俱出上蔡东门逐狡兔，岂可得乎？" According to his biography in the *Records of the Grand Historian*, before his execution, the Qin dynasty Chief Minister Li Si said to his son: "I would like to go with you again to hunt rabbits with our yellow dogs out of the eastern gate at Shangcai, but how can that be possible?"

三

劳谦寡悔,
忠信可久安。
劳谦寡悔,
忠信可久安。
天道害盈,
好胜者残。
强梁致灾,
多事招患。
欲得安乐,
独有无愆。
歌以言之,
忠信可久安。

3

Diligence and modesty leave one with few regrets,

loyalty and trust will make for lasting security.

Diligence and modesty leave one with few regrets,

loyalty and trust will make for lasting security.

The way of Heaven detests excessiveness,

belligerence causes its own destruction.

The powerful bring harm to themselves,

over-reaching always leads to damage.

If one desires peace and joy,

to commit no error is the only path.

I sing to make it clear:

loyalty and trust will make for lasting security.

四

役神者弊,
极欲令人枯。
役神者弊,
极欲令人枯。
颜回短折,
下及童乌。
纵体淫恣,
莫不早徂。
酒色何物,
自令不辜。
歌以言之,
酒色令人枯。

4

Those who labor their spirits get worn out,
excessive desire will make one wither.
Those who labor their spirits get worn out,
excessive desire will make one wither.
Yan Hui[1] died while still a young man,
just like Yang Xiong's boy Tongwu[2].
If a man gives way to complete abandon
he will meet an untimely death.
What is wine and sensuality
that makes such senseless victims of us?
I sing to make it clear:
Wine and sensuality make one wither.

---

1 颜回是孔子的学生。Yan Hui was a student of Confucius.
2 童乌是汉代著名学者扬雄之子。Tongwu was the son of Yang Xiong (53–18 BCE), a renowned scholar during the Han dynasty.

五

绝智弃学,
游心于玄默。
绝智弃学,
游心于玄默。
遇过而悔,
当不自得。
垂钓一壑,
所乐一国。
被发行歌,
和气四塞。
歌以言之,
游心于玄默。

5

Cut off wisdom and abandon learning,
let your heart roam amidst nothingness.

Cut off wisdom and abandon learning,
let your heart roam amidst nothingness.

Do not regret a missed opportunity,
nor pride yourself on a lucky break.

Cast your hook in a valley stream,
such joy surpasses ruling a state.

Let down your hair and sing your song,
so its harmony fills the four corners.

I sing to make it clear:
let your heart roam amidst nothingness.

六

思与王乔,
乘云游八极。
思与王乔,
乘云游八极。
凌厉五岳,
忽行万亿。
授我神药,
自生羽翼。
呼吸太和,
炼形易色。
歌以言之,
思行游八极。

6

I long to be with Prince Qiao the Immortal

and ride a cloud to the edge of Heaven.

I long to be with Prince Qiao the Immortal

and ride a cloud to the edge of Heaven.

We would hover above the Five Peaks,

crossing the cosmos in an instant.

He would give me a divine elixir,

causing feathered wings to sprout.

I would breathe the primordial air,

refining my body, adapting my color.

I sing to make it clear:

I wish to go to the edge of Heaven.

七

徘徊钟山,
息驾于层城。
徘徊钟山,
息驾于层城。
上荫华盖,
下采若英。
受道王母,
遂升紫庭。
逍遥天衢,
千载长生。
歌以言之,
徘徊于层城。

7

We hover above the godly Mt. Kunlun,

and rest our retinue at its peak.

We hover above the godly Mt. Kunlun,

and rest our retinue at its peak.

A colorful canopy spreads above us,

down below we pick pollia flowers.

The Queen Mother[1] guides our passage,

and soon we all ascend to the Purple Court[2].

We saunter along the road of Heaven,

enjoying our life of thousand years.

I sing to make it clear:

we hover above the peak of Mt. Kunlun.

---

1 王母，即西王母，传说中的女神。Queen Mother, also known as Queen Mother of the West, is a deity in Chinese mythology.
2 紫庭为道教中神仙及天帝之所居。Purple Court is where the deities reside in religious Taoism.

幽愤诗

嗟余薄祜,
少遭不造。
哀茕靡识,
越在襁褓。
母兄鞠育,
有慈无威。
恃爱肆姐,
不训不师。
爰及冠带,
凭宠自放。
抗心希古,
任其所尚。

Pent-up Sorrow[1]

Pitiful indeed was my lot,
misfortune found me as a child.
Unaware of grief and loneliness,
I fell from the infant bundle.
My mother and brother raised and nourished me,
showing love but no authority.
Thus I was abandoned to love,
but learned no self-discipline.
When I grew up, and took the cap and belt,[2]
I yielded to self-abandon.
My heart aspired to the Ancients,
and clung to those I most admire.

---

1 此诗作于狱中。嵇康与吕安、吕巽兄弟友善。吕巽与吕安妻子私通,然后诬告吕安不孝并将之下狱。应吕安之请,嵇康为其出庭作证。嵇康在朝中政敌借此也将其下狱,并将其与吕安一并处死。This poem was written in prison. Ji Kang was a friend of the brothers Lü An and Lü Xun. The latter had an affair with his brother's wife, and then turned around to accuse An of being unfilial and had him imprisoned. In defending himself, An solicited Ji Kang's help, upon which Ji Kang stepped forward for his friend. His political enemies took this opportunity to put Ji Kang in jail, too. Both Ji Kang and Lü An were executed.

2 古代男子二十岁加冠带,以表示成人。In ancient China, when a boy reached the age of twenty, he would receive cap and belt to wear to indicate his entrance into adulthood.

托好老庄,
贱物贵身。
志在守朴,
养素全真。
曰余不敏,
好善闇人。
子玉之败,
屡增惟尘。
大人含弘,
藏垢怀耻。
民之多僻,
政不由己。
惟此褊心,
显明臧否。
感悟思愆,
怛若创痏。
欲寡其过,
谤议沸腾。

I embraced the teachings of Lao-Zhuang,[1]

and valued life, ignoring gains.

I strove to keep my simplicity,

cultivating innocence and truth.

Some say I am not quick-minded,

that I care for virtue but know nothing of Man.

When Ziyu failed his task,[2]

dust piled up on his patron.

A great man needs a magnificent heart

to cover the dirt, and embrace shame.

When people behave perversely,

a leader has lost his control.

How narrow must be my own mind

to insist on the right and the wrong!

I have learned from my past mistake,

it pains me like a wound.

I was hoping to avoid further error,

yet slanders boiled and thrived.

---

1 这里指老子、庄子，道家思想的奠基人。Laozi and Zhuangzi are the founders of Taoist philosophy.
2 此句引用《左传·僖公二十七年》的一个典故。楚国大臣子文不顾他人劝告，推荐子玉为将。后子玉率军攻打晋国，兵败。This line alludes to a historical event in antiquity. When Ziwen recommended Ziyu to lead an army, people warned him of Ziyu's incompetence, but he ignored their advice; eventually, Ziyu suffered a defeat when leading an assault on another state.

性不伤物,
频致怨憎。
昔惭柳惠,
今愧孙登。
内负宿心,
外恧良朋。
仰慕严郑,
乐道闲居。
与世无营,
神气晏如。
咨予不淑,
婴累多虞。
匪降自天,
寔由顽疏。
理弊患结,
卒致囹圄。
对答鄙讯,
絷此幽阻。

By nature I would hurt nothing,

yet this has caused frequent resentment.

Ashamed in the past of Liu Hui[1],

today I am embarrassed by Sun Deng[2].

My heart knows I have failed myself,

and I am ashamed to face my friends.

The hermits Yan and Zheng[3] were admirable,

for their carefree delight in the Way!

They had no dealings with the world,

their minds and manners were at ease.

Alas, I have been so unwise,

to let myself be so ensnared by anxieties!

They were not sent down from Heaven,

but resulted from my foolishness.

Petition denied, misfortune followed,

till at last I was thrown into jail.

Facing their interrogations,

tied up in this dark confinement,

---

1 柳惠，即柳下惠，春秋时期鲁国一位正直大夫。Liu Hui, also known as Liu Xiahui, was an upright statesman in antiquity.
2 孙登为当时著名隐士，曾劝嵇康回避世事。Sun Deng was a renowned recluse at Ji Kang's time; he had advised Ji Kang to avoid worldly affairs.
3 严郑，即严君平、郑子真，汉代两位隐士。Yan and Zheng were two hermits during the previous Han dynasty.

实耻讼冤,
时不我与。
虽曰义直,
神辱志沮。
澡身沧浪,
岂云能补?
嗈嗈鸣雁,
奋翼北游。
顺时而动,
得意忘忧。
嗟我愤叹,
曾莫能俦。
事与愿违,
遘兹淹留。
穷达有命,
亦又何求?
古人有言,
善莫近名。
奉时恭默,
咎悔不生。
万石周慎,

how ashamed am I by this wrongful case!
Time is indeed against me.
Although I am an upright man,
insult and frustration knock me down.
Even if I may wash myself in a clear river,
how can I ever reverse the damage?
"*Yong... yong...*" – the geese cry in harmony,
as they spread their wings to the north.
They make their move with nature,
happy and unrestrained!
I release my sighs of bitterness,
unequal as I am to them.
Things turned out against my will,
and thus I languish.
Poverty and prosperity lie with Providence,
what then is left for me to wish for?
The Ancients made it clear,
that virtue doesn't lead to fame.
Quietly abide your time with reverence,
and guilt and regret will never rise.
Wan Dan was prudent and thoughtful,[1]

---

1 万石，即石奋，汉代一官吏，与其子皆谨慎为官处事，得使家业兴隆。Wan Dan, also known as Shi Fen, was a successful official during the Han dynasty. He and his four sons were all known as prudent and careful officials, which brought success and prosperity to their family.

安亲保荣。
世务纷纭,
祇搅予情。
安乐必诫,
乃终利贞。
煌煌灵芝,
一年三秀。
予独何为,
有志不就?
惩难思复,
心焉内疚。
庶勖将来,
无馨无臭。
采薇山阿,
散发岩岫。
永啸长吟,
颐性养寿。

bringing peace and glory to his family.

Worldly affairs are mere chaos!

I must examine my feelings with care.

If you are careful with comfort and pleasure,

happiness will be yours in the end.

Brilliant are those magical mushrooms,

that bloom three times a year.

What is the matter with me,

to leave my wish unfulfilled?

I would learn lessons from the past,

yet my heart is fraught with guilt.

I wish to do better in the future,

leaving behind no stench of infamy or fame.

I would pick my ferns by the hillside,

and let down my hair in the cave.

I would whistle and chant without stopping,

forever nurture my spirit and life!

四言赠兄秀才入军十八章

一

鸳鸯于飞,
肃肃其羽。
朝游高原,
夕宿兰渚。
邕邕和鸣,
顾眄俦侣。
俛仰慷慨,
优游容与。

A Tetrasyllabic Poem on Seeing Off My Brother the Cultivated Talent to Join the Army (in eighteen stanzas)

1

The mandarin ducks take to the air:

"*su... su...*", their whistling wings.

Throughout the morning they crest the plateau,

at dusk they rest on the violet marsh.

"*Yong... yong...*", their harmonious call,

glancing sideways at their companions.

Upwards and downwards they float in deep affection,

carefree and at ease.

二

鸳鸯于飞,
啸侣命俦。
朝游高原,
夕宿中洲。
交颈振翼,
容与清流。
咀嚼兰蕙,
俛仰优游。

2

The mandarin ducks are in flight

and calling on their mates.

Throughout the morning they crest the plateau,

at dusk they come to rest on the middle isle.

They twine their necks together and spread their wings,

lazily float on the clear stream.

They savor the violet and the sweet clover,

sauntering up and down.

三

泳彼长川,
言息其浒。
陟彼高冈,
言刈其楚。
嗟我征迈,
独行踽踽。
仰彼凯风,
涕泣如雨。

3

They swim in the long river,

and rest themselves on its banks.

I stride up that high hill,

slashing its thorns before me.

Alas, my journey is long,

trudging along on my own.

My face is turned to the southern breeze;[1]

my tears fall like rain.

1　"凯风"比喻亲情，取自《诗经·邶风》："凯风自南，吹彼棘心。" "Gentle south wind" is a metaphor for domestic love; see poem 32 in *The Shijing* or *The Book of Poetry*: "The gentle wind from the south/ Blows on the heart of thorn bushes."

四

泳彼长川,
言息其沚。
陟彼高冈,
言刈其杞。
嗟我独征,
靡瞻靡恃。
仰彼凯风,
载坐载起。

4

They swim in the long river,

and rest themselves on its banks.

I walk up that tall hill,

slashing its thorns before me.

Alas my journey is long,

with no one to care or help me along.

My face is turned to the southern breeze,

I rest and rise again without ceasing.

五

穆穆惠风,
扇彼轻尘。
奕奕素波,
转此游鳞。
伊我之劳,
有怀佳人。
寤言永思,
寔钟所亲。

5

Calm and mild the breeze,

with its light dust drifting.

Brilliant, bright, the white waves

twisting and turning the fishes' scales.

My heart is filled with anxieties

for the one I love.

My mind works long into the night,

thinking only of my beloved.

六

所亲安在?
舍我远迈。
弃此荪芷,
袭彼萧艾。
虽曰幽深,
岂无颠沛?
言念君子,
不遐有害。

6

Where is the man I care about?
He has left me to go on a long journey.
He has abandoned these scented angelicas,
and put on the mugwort plants.¹
However deeply he may conceal himself,
how can he avoid all peril?
Gentleman, I cherish you,
and pray you will meet no harm.

---

1 这两行出自《离骚》："何昔日之芳草兮，今直为此萧艾也。"嵇康以此提示，其兄参军无异于放弃自己的人格与初衷。These two lines refer to Qu Yuan's "Lisao" or "Encountering Sorrow": "How the scented plants in the past,/ have become today's mugworts?" Ji Kang is suggesting that his brother's decision to join the army amounts to abandoning his integrity.

七

人生寿促,
天地长久。
百年之期,
孰云其寿?
思欲登仙,
以济不朽。
揽辔踟蹰,
仰顾我友。

7

Man's life is brief,

Heaven and Earth endure forever.

We expect a hundred years of life,

but who can actually live that long?

I may wish to rise and become a god,

to arrive at immortality.

Yet, hands on bridle, I pull up my horse,

and turn around to seek my friend.

八

我友焉之？
隔兹山冈。
谁谓河广，
一苇可航。
徒恨永离，
逝彼路长。
瞻仰弗及，
徙倚彷徨。

8

Where is my friend going?

Beyond the top of this hill.

Who said the width of the river

could be crossed on a mere reed?[1]

In vain I regret our separation,

alas, his road will be long.

I look, but cannot see its end;

halting, up and down I walk.

---

[1] 这两行取自《诗经·卫风》:"谁谓河广,一苇杭之。"此处嵇康反用其意,谓很难再与兄相见。These two lines are from poem 61 of *The Shijing* or *The Book of Poetry*: "Who says the River is wide? / A reed may cross it." Ji Kang here turns them around to emphasize the opposite, that it would be very hard to see his brother again.

九

良马既闲,
丽服有晖。
左揽繁弱,
右接忘归。
风驰电逝,
蹑景追飞。
凌厉中原,
顾盼生姿。

9

Our fine horses take their rest,
our brilliant clothes shine bright.
I take up my bow in my left hand,
draw out an arrow with my right.
I dash about like wind and lightning,
flying, running after the sunlight,
galloping over the wide terrain,
looking back with wild eyes.

十

携我好仇,
载我轻车。
南凌长阜,
北厉清渠。
仰落惊鸿,
俯引渊鱼。
盘于游畋,
其乐只且。

10

Together with my good companion,

we go for a ride in my light carriage.

We charge right over the southern mound,

to the north we cross the clear canal.

We bring down a startled goose with our arrows,

and take a fish from the river's depth.

We delight ourselves in hunting,

and oh, to speak of our joy!

十一

凌高远眄,
俯仰咨嗟。
怨彼幽絷,
邈尔路遐。
虽有好音,
谁与清歌?
虽有姝颜,
谁与发华?
仰讯高云,
俯托轻波。
乘流远遁,
抱恨山阿。

11

We climb on high and look far away,

rising, falling, chanting, and sighing.

How I resent your deep confinement,[1]

the road you travel, how remote!

I may be able to hold a tune,

but who can share my clear song?

I may have a pretty appearance,

but to whom can I show off my good looks?

I speak to the clouds in the sky,

entrust my feelings to the gentle waters.

I would ride the river to escape,

hold my resentment close in a hill's nook.

---

1 此指其兄在军中的职务。This is a reference to his brother's post in the army.

十二

轻车迅迈,
息彼长林。
春木载荣,
布叶垂阴。
习习谷风,
吹我素琴。
咬咬黄鸟,
顾俦弄音。
感悟驰情,
思我所钦。
心之忧矣,
永啸长吟。

12

The light carriages travel swiftly,

now they take their rest by the long groves.

The Spring plants are flourishing here,

spreading the shade of their leaves.

Gently flows the wind from the valley

across the strings of my plain zither.

The yellow birds are chirruping,

seeking mates with their songs.

I am moved, my feelings gallop fast

in pursuit of the one I admire.

My heart is sorrowful, and

for a long time I whistle and chant.

十三

浩浩洪流,
带我邦畿。
萋萋绿林,
奋荣扬晖。
鱼龙瀺灂,
山鸟群飞。
驾言出游,
日夕忘归。
思我良朋,
如渴如饥。
愿言不获,
怆矣其悲。

13

Torrential are the currents of the river,

a belt across the region of the capital.

Lush are its green groves,

displaying their brilliant blossoms.

Fish and dragon leap and splash,

mountain birds flock in the sky.

I go for a ride in my carriage,

forgetting to return at dusk.

How I miss my good friend,

as if pained by hunger and thirst!

But my wish is not to be granted,

and so my heart is torn and grieved.

十四

息徒兰圃,
秣马华山。
流磻平皋,
垂纶长川。
目送归鸿,
手挥五弦。
俯仰自得,
游心太玄。
嘉彼钓叟,
得鱼忘筌。
郢人逝矣,
谁与尽言?

14

We take a rest on the violet field,

and feed our horses along the flowery hill.

We shoot arrows across the moor,

cast our lines on the long stream.

My eyes see off the returning geese,

my fingers pluck the five-stringed zither.

Up and down, to my heart's content,

I let my mind roam through the Great Mystery.

How greatly I honor that fisherman

who, catching the fish, forgets the trap.[1]

The man from Ying is gone forever,

with whom can I share my word again?[2]

---

1   这两行用了《庄子·外物》中的典故："筌者所以在鱼，得鱼而忘筌……言者所以在意，得意而忘言。吾安得夫忘言之人而与之言哉！" This is an allusion to a passage in *Zhuangzi*: "the purpose of a fish trap is to catch fish; as soon as a fish is caught one forgets the trap... the purpose of a word is to express meaning; as soon as the meaning is caught one forgets the word. Where can I find one who forgets the word so that I can converse with him!"

2   "郢人"取自《庄子·徐无鬼》，比喻知音或知己。This is another allusion to the book of *Zhuangzi*. The "man from Ying" is a metaphor for a friend with whom one can share one's feelings and thought, someone who "knows the tune."

十五

闲夜肃清,
朗月照轩。
微风动袿,
组帐高褰。
旨酒盈樽,
莫与交欢。
鸣琴在御,
谁与鼓弹?
仰慕同趣,
其馨若兰。
佳人不存,
能不永叹?

15

The night is calm and clear,

the moon shines brightly on the porch.

A gentle breeze touches my sleeves,

high, high is the decorated curtain.

Fine wine fills the goblets,

but there is none to share the pleasure.

The singing zither lies at my side,

with whom can I enjoy its music?

I would cherish one with similar taste,

our conversation would be like scented violet.[1]

But he that I love is not here with me,

how can I stifle my sighing?

---

[1] 这两行取自《易·系辞上》："同心之言，其臭如兰。" This is an allusion to the *Yijing* or *The Book of Change*: "the words of people with similar minds are as fragrant as the violet."

十六

乘风高游,
远登灵丘。
托好松乔,
携手俱游。
朝发太华,
夕宿神州。
弹琴咏诗,
聊以忘忧。

16

I ride the wind to roam on high,
and climb the distant sacred hill.

Entrusting myself to the Immortals,
hand in hand we wander together.

We depart Mount Taihua in the morning;
at dusk we take our rest in the godly land.

We pluck our zithers and chant poetry;
and, for a moment, put aside our worries.

十七

琴诗自乐,
远游可珍。
含道独往,
弃智遗身。
寂乎无累,
何求于人?
长寄灵岳,
怡志养神。

17

I please myself with music and poetry,

and roaming far is also to be treasured.

Holding the Way I take my own path,

leaving behind both knowledge and the body.

Serene and free from burden,

what do I have to ask of others?

I find my permanent lodging high on a sacred peak,

there to nourish my spirit and will.

十八

流俗难悟,
逐物不还。
至人远鉴,
归之自然。
万物为一,
四海同宅。
与彼共之,
予何所惜!
生若浮寄,
暂见忽终。
世故纷纭,
弃之八戎。
泽雉虽饥,
不愿园林。
安能服御,
劳形苦心?
身贵名贱,
荣辱何在?
贵得肆志,
纵心无悔。

18

The people of this world are blinded,

chasing things they cannot catch.

The Perfect Man sees far into future,

and knows he must come back to nature.

The myriad things are only one,

the Four Seas the same residence.

I share all I own with them;

what is there for me to regret?

Human life is but a fleeting sojourn,

beheld for a moment, then suddenly vanished.

Worldly affairs are harum-scarum,

let's escape to the remote regions.

A marsh pheasant, however hungry,

would not want to live in a walled estate.

Would a man choose to haul a chariot

belaboring his body and embittering his heart?

Rich and noble, poor and humble,

where do we find our glory and our shame?

True treasure is found in following our will,

to free ourselves, and gratify our hearts.

五言赠秀才诗

双鸾匿景曜,
戢翼太山崖。
抗首漱朝露,
晞阳振羽仪。
长鸣戏云中,
时下息兰池。
自谓绝尘埃,
终始永不亏。
何意世多艰,
虞人来我疑。
云网塞四区,
高罗正参差。
奋迅势不便。
六翮无所施。
隐姿就长缨,
卒为时所羁。
单雄翩孤逝,
哀吟伤生离。
徘徊恋俦侣,
慷慨高山陂。

A Pentasyllabic Poem to My Brother the Cultivated Talent

Twin cranes, hiding their brilliant plumage,

gather their wings by Mount Tai's cliffs,

raise their heads to swallow the morning dew,

expose to the sun their out-stretched feathers,

call at length at play in the clouds,

and come to rest by the violet pond.

They feel cut off from the dust of the world,

never to meet its danger and its damage.

Alas, how the world teems with many perils!

The fowlers come out to stalk us:

They set up nets all over like clouds,

spreading their tall traps here and there.

No longer can we roam or soar,

our forceful wings can find no place to spread.

Hiding our nature we come to the long rope,

surrendering ourselves to the rules of the time.

The male bird dashes away on his lone path,

grieving and crying over this lifetime departure.

Hovering, his thought goes out to his companion,

in deep sorrow, above the high slope of the mountain.

Ji Kang

鸟尽良弓藏,
谋极身心危。
吉凶虽在己,
世路多崄巇。
安得反初服,
抱玉宝六奇。
逍遥游太清,
携手长相随。

When the birds are gone, the good bow is put away,
once ideas end, the aide's life is put in danger.[1]
Even though fortune and disaster lie with us,
the world's roads are full of ups and downs.
How can we go back to our original clothing,
to treasure our jade and sharpen our wits?
Let us wander freely in the Great Clearing,[2]
forever accompany each other, hand in hand!

---

1 这两行用了《史记·淮阴侯列传》中的典故；韩信临死前说："狡兔死，良狗烹；高鸟尽，良弓藏；敌国破，谋臣亡。"This alludes to the fate of Han Xin (231–196 BCE). Before he was executed by Emperor Gaozu of the Han dynasty, he cried out: "When the fast-running rabbit is dead, the good dog is cooked; when the high-flying bird is finished, the good bow is put away; when the enemy's state is defeated, aides and advisers are dead."

2 太清，指天空，也指天道。The Great Clearing refers to the sky, also the Way of Heaven.

酒会诗

乐哉苑中游,
周览无穷已。
百卉吐芳华,
崇基邈高跱。
林木纷交错,
玄池戏鲂鲤。
轻丸毙翔禽,
纤纶出鳣鲔。
坐中发美赞,
异气同音轨。
临川献清酤,
微歌发皓齿。
素琴挥雅操,
清声随风起。
斯会岂不乐?
恨无东野子。
酒中念幽人,
守故弥终始。
但当体七弦,
寄心在知己。

A Party Poem

Happily we roam and saunter in the park,

and look across this vast, this endless land.

A hundred flowers blossom in fragrance,

tall platforms in the distance, remote and high.

Trees twist and intertwine profusely,

breams and carps sport in the pond.

A flying bird is killed by light pellet,

a silken line hauls in the sturgeon.

Everyone present shouts their praises,

their many voices rising in unison.

We offer our fresh wine by the river,

listen to sweet songs from between white teeth.

Plain zithers send out elegant tunes,

clear songs rise and fall with the wind.

Who can say this party is not joyful?

but my friend Dongye is not alongside me.

As I drink I miss that reclusive person,

our old feelings will persist forever.

Let me pick up the seven-string zither,

entrusting my heart to him, the connoisseur.

Ji Kang

述志诗二首

一

潜龙育神躯,
濯鳞戏兰池。
延颈慕大庭,
寝足俟皇羲。
庆云未垂景,
盘桓朝阳陂。
悠悠非吾匹,
圭步应俗宜。
殊类难遍周,
鄙议纷流离。
轗轲丁悔吝,
雅志不得施。
耕耨感宁越,
马席激张仪。

Expressing My Will: Two Poems

1

The hidden dragon cultivates his luminous body,
bathing and sporting in the violet pond.
Stretching my neck I long for Da Ting, the ancient ruler,
resting my feet, I await the legendary Fu Xi.
The shadows of the crimson clouds have yet to descend
as they hang above the slope beneath the morning sun.
Those Ancients are not to be my companions after all,
so let me carefully follow what custom decrees.
Different in kind, I can't meet everyone's demand,
and harsh criticism is widespread.
Through ups and downs I fall upon misfortune;
no way for my natural will to be fulfilled.
Tilling and ploughing caused Ning Yue to change his fate,
a horse's saddle urged Zhang Yi to take up his post.[1]

---

[1] 这两行用了两个战国时期的历史典故。宁越曾是普通农民，苦于农事之劳，后经勤奋学习得以成为周威公的老师。张仪曾被苏秦让座于马席，因感羞辱而发奋成为秦相。These two lines use two historical allusions. Ning Yue, who was a commoner, was pained by harsh farm labor; through diligent studies he was able to become the tutor of a feudal prince. Zhang Yi, feeling insulted by Su Qin who had offered a horse saddle for him to sit on, eventually took upon himself the post of a minister for the state of Qin.

逝将离群侣,
杖策追洪崖。
焦明振六翮,
罗者安所羁?
浮游太清中,
更求新相知。
比翼翔云汉,
饮露餐琼枝。
多念世间人,
凤驾咸驱驰。
冲静得自然,
荣华安足为。

I will take my leave of the madding crowd,

and staff in hand I will follow Hongya the immortal.

When a phoenix strongly plies his wings,

how can the fowler hope to catch him?

He hovers and roams in the Great Clearing,

seeking new companions and friends.

We soar above the clouds, wing touching wing,

drink dew and dine on gemstone boughs.

Have pity on the people of the world!

Each day they rise so early in pursuit of one another.

Peace and emptiness lead one to nature,

glory and wealth are not worth chasing!

Ji Kang

二

斥鷃擅蒿林,
仰笑神凤飞。
坎井蟠蛙宅,
神龟安所归?
恨自用身拙,
任意多永思。
远实与世殊,
义誉非所希。
往事既已谬,
来者犹可追。
何为人事间,
自令心不夷?
慷慨思古人,
梦想见容辉。
愿与知己遇,
舒愤启其微。
岩穴多隐逸,
轻举求吾师。
晨登箕山巅,

2

Quails have taken control of the wormwood bushes,
they laugh at the soaring godly phoenix.
Beetles and frogs reside in shallow wells,
where will the godly turtle find his place?
I regret the awkward way I conduct myself;
often I am too thoughtful and stubborn.
Far from reality, removed from the world,
I care little for righteousness and fame.
Mistakes have been made in the past,
yet I still have hopes for the future.
Why must I fret about worldly affairs,
making my heart so ill at ease?
In deepest thought I turn to the Ancients,
and long for a glimpse of their brilliant faces.
I wish to meet with an understanding friend,
to relieve my distress and share his mystery.
Rocks and caves attract many a hermit,
I would fly there to seek my masters.
I would ascend Mount Ji in the morning,[1]

---

1 箕山为古代隐士许由隐居之处。Mount Ji is where the ancient hermit Xu You was said to have lived.

日夕不知饥。
玄居养营魄,
千载长自绥。

and even at dusk I would feel no hunger.

I would hide in the darkness to nourish my soul,

and to live in peace for a thousand years!

答二郭三首

一

天下悠悠者,
下京趋上京。
二郭怀不群,
超然来北征。
乐道托菜庐,
雅志无所营。
良时遘其愿,
遂结欢爱情。
君子义是亲,
恩好笃平生。
寡智自生灾,
屡使众衅成。
豫子匿梁侧,
聂政变其形。

In Reply to the Two Guos: Three Poems

1

Look at those bustling crowds under the sky,

swarming from the lower to the upper capital!

The two Guos embrace a different kind of mind,

they journeyed north to my remote home.

In a thatched hut they find delight in the Way,

their noble minds leave nothing else to seek.

Our mutual wish was granted in good time,

we developed a deep and loving bond.

Gentlemen are devoted to friendship,

true affection will last till the end of life.

Lack of wisdom leads to misfortune,

it often brings about calamity.

Yu Rang[1] hid himself under the bridge,

Nie Zheng[2] destroyed his face when his task was done.

---

1 豫子，即豫让，战国时刺客，曾躲在桥下刺杀主人的仇敌，未遂，自杀。Yu Rang was an ancient assassin, who hid himself under the bridge to assassinate his patron's enemy. Having failed, he committed suicide.

2 聂政为另一战国时刺客。他在刺杀了主人的仇敌后，为隐瞒证据毁形自杀。Nie Zheng was another ancient assassin. After killing his patron's enemy, he first destroyed his face, so that people wouldn't be able to recognize him, and then committed suicide.

顾此怀怛惕,
虑在苟自宁。
今当寄他域,
严驾不得停。
本图终宴婉,
今更不克并。
二子赠嘉诗,
馥如幽兰馨。
恋土思所亲,
能不气愤盈?

Thinking about them makes me fearful,
all I want is to make myself secure.
Now I am moving to another region,
preparing my cart so it will not falter.
We have wanted to be together forever,
now we are forced to abandon that hope.
Both of you sent me your gracious poems,
they are fragrant as the hidden violets.
We are all attached to homes and friends;
ah, my heart is flooded with feelings!

二

昔蒙父兄祚,
少得离负荷。
因疏遂成懒,
寝迹北山阿。
但愿养性命,
终己靡有他。
良辰不我期,
当年值纷华。
坎𡒄趣世务,
常恐婴网罗。
羲农邈已远,
拊膺独咨嗟。
朔戒贵尚容,
渔父好扬波。
虽逸亦已难,
非余心所嘉。
岂若翔区外,
餐琼漱朝霞。
遗物弃鄙累,

2

Blessed with a good father and brother,

I rarely carried a heavy load.

But sloth descended into indolence,

and I hid myself away on the north slope.

I just wanted to nourish my life,

self-fulfillment my only goal.

I met with no auspicious moment,

but lived through a time of chaos.

Reluctantly I followed the world's demands,

fearful of being caught up in its nets.

The times of the Ancients are truly remote,

clapping my chest, I utter my lonely sighs.

Dongfang Shuo[1] told his son to value conformity,

the fisherman bobs up and down on the waves.

Their views may sound easy, but are hard in practice,

neither of them is close to my heart's desire.

The best thing is to hover above the world,

dining on gemstones, rinsed with the clouds of dawn,

abandoning ignoble burdens,

---

1 东方朔为汉代著名朝臣与文学家。Dongfang Shuo (154-93BCE) was a famous courtier and writer in the Han dynasty.

逍遥游太和。
结友集灵岳,
弹琴登清歌。
有能从此者,
古人岂足多?

roaming free in the Great Harmony,

gathering together on the godly peaks,

playing upon zithers, letting clear songs arise.

If we can find those who can act this way,

the Ancients can no longer be worthy of praise!

三

详观凌世务,
屯险多忧虞。
施报更相市,
大道匿不舒。
夷路殖枳棘,
安步将焉如?
权智相倾夺,
名位不可居。
鸾凤避罻罗,
远托昆仑墟。
庄周悼灵龟,

3

Take a careful look at the world's disorder,

dangers pile up, shock upon terror,

everyone trading favors and paybacks,

the great Way hidden from view.

Thorns and brambles grow across level roads,

where can I wander and take my leisure?

People brandish their intelligence and power,

but fame and rank can never be trusted.

The phoenix struggles free of the net,

and flies all the way to Mount Kunlun.

Zhuangzi lamented the sacred turtle,[1]

---

1 此行用《庄子·秋水》篇中如下典故：庄子钓于濮水，楚王使大夫二人往先焉，曰："愿以境内累矣！"庄子持竿不顾，曰："吾闻楚有神龟，死已三千岁矣，王巾笥而藏之庙堂之上。此龟者，宁其死为留骨而贵乎？宁其生而曳尾于涂中乎？"二大夫曰："宁生而曳尾涂中。"庄子曰："往矣！吾将曳尾于涂中。" In the "Autumn Waters" of the *Zhuangzi*, the King of Chu sent two officials to ask Zhuangzi to rule the land. Zhuangzi, who was fishing, said, "I have heard of a godly turtle, which has been dead for three thousand years. The king put it in a bamboo box and hid it in the temple. So for this turtle, would it rather be a noble dead bone, or be alive and drag its tail on the road?" The two officials answered, "it would rather be alive and drag its tail on the road." Zhuangzi then said, "Be gone! For I would rather drag my tail on the road."

越稷嗟王舆。
至人存诸己,
隐璞乐玄虚。
功名何足殉,
乃欲列简书?
所好亮若兹,
杨氏叹交衢。
去去从所志,
敢谢道不俱。

Yue Sou sighed over his princely carriage.[1]
A perfect man finds fulfillment in his own self,
he hides his nature and delights in mystery.
Why would he sacrifice for fame and glory,
to have his name inscribed on bamboo slips?[2]
If this is indeed what man treasures,
Mr. Yang Zhu had reason to sigh at the crossroads.[3]
Let me take my leave and follow my will,
forgive me that our ways are not the same.

1　《庄子·让王》篇记载，越人三世弑其君，后请王子搜为君。王子搜逃进山洞。越人烧艾草将其熏出。王子搜无奈，只得登车而返。上车后，他叹道："君乎！君乎！独不可以舍我乎？" In the "Abdicating Kingship" chapter of the *Zhuangzi*, Prince Sou of the Yue, having seen three earlier kings killed, escaped to a cave. The people of the Yue burned wormwood to smoke him out and offered him the princely carriage. Yue Sou, while climbing on the carriage, sighed, facing the sky, "Prince, Prince, why does it have to be me!"

2　郭遐周在赠与嵇康的诗中曾说："所贵身名存，功烈在简书。" Guo Xiaozhou, in his poem to Ji Kang, has written: "We value passing down our names to posterity, / and having our achievements inscribed on bamboo slips."

3　因人们面对歧路，常感到茫然无所措。（参见《列子·说符》） Because people may choose different roads and get lost. (See the "Shuo fu" chapter in the *Liezi*.)

与阮德如

含哀还旧庐,
感切伤心肝。
良时遘吾子,
谈慰臭如兰。
畴昔恨不早,
既面侔旧欢。
不悟卒永离,
念隔增忧叹。
事故无不有,
别易会良难。
郢人忽已逝,
匠石寝不言。
泽雉穷野草,
灵龟乐泥蟠。
荣名秽人身,
高位多灾患。
未若捐外累,
肆志养浩然。
颜氏希有虞,

To Ruan Deru

In sorrow I return to my old hut,

my body pierced, my heart in tatters.

I met you, my friend, at a good time,

our conversations held the fragrance of violets.

We regretted having not met earlier,

but once together we were like old friends.

I never thought you would be leaving so soon,

now the long separation before us deepens my grief.

The unforeseen can surely arise at any time,

but once apart, reunion is hard to imagine.

When the man from Ying was suddenly gone,

the stone smith forever ceased his work.[1]

Marsh pheasants live out their span among wild grass,

the godly turtle prefers to saunter in the mud.

Fame and glory defile our bodies,

high rank brings about many calamities.

Better to abandon all external burdens,

and devote to nourishing our cosmic life energy.

Yan Hui[2] aspired after Shun, the ancient ruler,

---

1 郢人、匠石是《庄子·徐无鬼》篇中的两位知己。The man from Ying and stone smith are intimate friends in the book of *Zhuangzi*.
2 颜回为孔子得意门生。Yan Hui was Confucius' favorite disciple.

鵬子慕黄轩。
涓彭独何人？
唯志在所安。
渐渍殉近欲，
一往不可攀。
生生在豫积。
勿以恨自宽。
南土旱不凉，
衿计宜早完。
君其爱德素，
行路慎风寒。
自力致所怀，
临文情辛酸。

Xi Peng[1] uttered his admiration for the Yellow Emperor.

What kind of men are Juan and Peng, the immortals?

They only follow the dictates of their heart.

If we get lost pursuing our immediate desire,

once gone, we can never retrieve ourselves.

Life needs cultivation at every juncture,

never seek comfort in luck's allure!

The southern land is dry, not cool,

so please think early about your plan.

Take a good care of your virtue, Sir,

and be careful with the weather on the road.

I have done my best to express my feelings,

facing the poem, my heart is sore and torn.

---

1 隰朋为春秋时齐国大夫。Xi Peng was an official in the state of Qi during the Spring and Autumn era.

四言诗

一

淡淡流水,
沦胥而逝。
泛泛柏舟,
载浮载滞。
微啸清风,
鼓檝容裔。
放棹投竿,
优游卒岁。

Tetrasyllabic Verses[1]

1

Smoothly, slowly flows the river,
folding together, it rolls away.
The cypress boat floats on and on,
drifting and stopping by turn.
I whistle gently in the soft breeze,
dipping the oars with ease.
Dropping the paddle I cast my rod,
living out my carefree life.

---

1 十一选三。Three out of eleven.

二

猗猗兰蔼,
殖彼中原。
绿叶幽茂,
丽蕊秾繁。
馥馥蕙芳,
顺风而宣。
将御椒房,
吐薰龙轩。
瞻彼秋草,
怅矣惟骞。

2

Lush and dense are the violets,

that grow on those central plains.

Their green leaves are luxuriantly dark,

their brilliant petals dense and profuse.

Sweet and balmy are the melilotuses,

spreading their aura on the wind.

They are cultivated to scent royal chambers,

and to perfume dragon carriages.

Look at those Autumn grasses,

how moved I am for their decline!

三

微风清扇,
云气四除。
皓皓亮月,
丽于高隅。
兴命公子,
携手同车。
龙骥翼翼,
扬镳踟蹰。
肃肃宵征,
造我友庐。
光灯吐辉,
华幔长舒。
鸾觞酌醴,
神鼎烹鱼。
弦超子野,
叹过绵驹。
流咏太素,

3

A gentle breeze is refreshing,

dispelling the cloud in all directions.

Brilliant is the gleaming moon,

displaying its beauty in a high corner.

Delighted, I ask a noble man

to ride in my carriage, hand in hand.

The dragon steed gallops in grandeur,

it pauses and halts as I pull the reins.

Swiftly I embark on my night journey,

to call on my friend at his cottage.

A brilliant lamp emits its glow,

the colorful curtains long unfolding.

We drink our wine from simurgh goblets,

and boil fish in a godly tripod.

Our zither-playing surpasses Ziye,

our singing overtakes Mian Ju.[1]

Glancing up, I chant on the Great Simplicity,

---

1 子野为古代著名乐师，绵驹为古代著名歌手。Ziye and Mian Ju are respectively famous musician and singer in the past.

俯赞玄虚。
孰克英贤,
与尔剖符。

looking down, I praise the Dark Emptiness.[1]

Who can be the outstanding worthy?

I will split and match a tally with you!

---

[1] 太素、玄虚均指道家思想中的"道",为万物之始。Great Simplicity and Dark Emptiness refer to the Dao, the ultimate origin and destiny of the universe.

思亲诗

奈何愁兮愁无聊,
恒恻恻兮心若抽。
愁奈何兮悲思多,
情郁结兮不可化。
奄失恃兮孤茕茕,
内自悼兮啼失声。
思报德兮邈已绝,
感鞠育兮情剥裂。
嗟母兄兮永潜藏,
想形容兮内摧伤。
感阳春兮思慈亲,
欲一见兮路无因。
望南山兮发哀叹,
感几杖兮涕汍澜。
念畴昔兮母兄在,
心逸豫兮寿四海。
忽已逝兮不可追,
心穷约兮但有悲。
上空堂兮廓无依,
睹遗物兮心崩摧。

Missing My Loved Ones

How can I cope with this grief that won't decline?
Long, long, it has been tormenting my heart.
Grief, it brings thought upon thought of such sorrow,
it knots my feelings, which I have no way to liberate.
Suddenly I lost my reliance, left abandoned and alone,
I lament inside myself, losing control of my voice.
I would repay their love, but they are cut off from me,
I feel obliged for their nurturing, my heart is split apart.
Alas, my mother and elder brother are forever hidden away,
how I miss their appearance, my whole being destroyed.
Moved by the sunny Springtime, I miss my loving ones,
how I want to see them again, but no road leads me there.
I gaze at the South Mountain[1], uttering my sad sighs,
seeing their armrests and canes, tears crisscrossing my face.
In the past, when my mother and brother were still alive,
my heart was peaceful and wide, like the four great oceans.
Suddenly they were gone, to never be seen again,
deprived of all sustenance, my heart knows only sorrow.
I ascend the deserted hall, my pillars have disappeared,
looking at the objects they left behind, my heart collapses.

---

1 南山是思亲与长寿的象征。South Mountain symbolizes longing for the loved ones and longevity.

中夜悲兮当告谁,
独抆泪兮抱哀戚。
日远迈兮思予心,
恋所生兮泪不禁。
慈母没兮谁与骄,
顾自怜兮心忉忉。
诉苍天兮天不闻,
泪如雨兮叹青云。
欲弃忧兮寻复来,
痛殷殷兮不可裁。

嵇康

Heartbroken at midnight, to whom can I tell my grief?

Alone I wipe my tears and embrace my sorrow.

The sun marches on, my heart is teeming with thought,

I long for my begetter, and I cannot stop my tears.

My loving mother gone, who is here to pamper me?

Turning inside, I pity myself and ah, my heart is grieved.

I appeal to the azure sky, but the sky does not hear,

my tears fall like rain, my sighs turn into blue clouds.

I want to banish my sorrows, but soon they return,

my pains are deep and piercing, they can never be stopped.

Ji Kang

六言诗

东方朔至清

外以贪污内贞,
秽身滑稽隐名。
不为世累所撄,
所以知足无营。

Hexasyllabic Verses[1]

Dongfang Shuo, The Ultimate Purity

On the outside he seemed foul and greedy, but within
    he was upright;
he sullied himself by playing a fool, thereby hiding his name.
Refusing to be caught up in the world's concerns,
he knew the way to self-fulfillment and non-striving.

---

1 十首选三。Three out of ten.

老莱妻贤名

不愿夫子相荆,
相将避禄隐耕。
乐道闲居采萍,
终厉高节不倾。

Laolai's Wife, A Virtuous Name[1]

She would not let her husband serve in the court of Chu,
together they avoided official fortune, hid away and ploughed the fields.
Delighting in the Way, living in leisure, picking the duckweeds,
right up to the end they never let their high integrity fall.

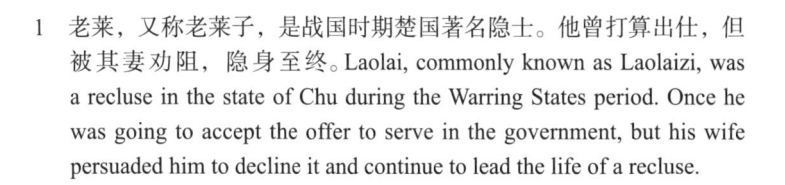

---

1   老莱，又称老莱子，是战国时期楚国著名隐士。他曾打算出仕，但被其妻劝阻，隐身至终。Laolai, commonly known as Laolaizi, was a recluse in the state of Chu during the Warring States period. Once he was going to accept the offer to serve in the government, but his wife persuaded him to decline it and continue to lead the life of a recluse.

嗟古贤原宪

弃背膏梁朱颜,
乐此屡空饥寒。
形陋体逸心宽,
得志一世无患。

In Praise of the Ancient Worthy Yuan Xian[1]

He cast aside delicious food and rouged faces,
and took delight in cold and the frequently empty bowl.
He looked shabby, but his body was easy, his mind free;
all his life he had his way without misfortune.

---

[1] 原宪是孔子的门生。Yuan Xian was a student of Confucius.

向 秀

Xiang Xiu

向秀（？—？），字子期，与嵇康、山涛为友。颇好老庄之学，并曾与嵇康辩论养生之术。嵇康被害后，向秀应召入朝廷任职。所作《思旧赋》乃唯一现存诗作，始终被认为是千古绝唱。

Xiang Xiu (?–?), courtesy name Ziqi, was a friend of Ji Kang and Shan Tao. He showed passion for the writings of Laozi and Zhuangzi, and once debated with Ji Kang on the art of alchemy and longevity. After Ji Kang's execution, he answered the summons of the court and became an official in the capital. His "Rhapsody on Recalling Old Friends" is his only extant poetic work; it has always been regarded as a masterpiece.

思旧赋（并序）

　　余与嵇康、吕安居止接近。其人并有不羁之才，然嵇志远而疏，吕心旷而放。其后各以事见法。嵇博综技艺，于丝竹特妙，临当就命，顾视日影，索琴而弹之。余逝将西迈，经其旧庐，于时日薄虞渊，寒冰凄然。邻人有吹笛者，发声寥亮。追思曩昔游宴之好，感音而叹，故作赋云：

将命适于远京兮，
遂旋反而北徂。
济黄河以泛舟兮，
经山阳之旧居。
瞻旷野之萧条兮，
息余驾乎城隅。
践二子之遗迹兮，
历穷巷之空庐。

Rhapsody on Recalling Old Friends
(with a Preface)

I once lived very close to Ji Kang and Lü An. Both of them had unbridled talent. Ji was lofty-minded but aloof, Lü had a great heart but lacked self-restraint. Later, they both ran foul of the law and were executed. Ji was well versed in many of the arts, especially in playing string and wind instruments. Before his execution, he looked back at his shadow under the sun and asked for a zither to play. Later, as I was headed to the west, I passed their old cottages. The sun was setting, it was icy cold and desolate. One of the neighbors was playing a flute, its sound far-reaching and shrill. Moved by this, I began to recall the joys of our outings and banquets in the past; sighing, I composed this rhapsody:

Following the official order, on route to the distant capital,
I turn round and head off to the north.
Taking a boat I cross the Yellow River,
passing their old residences at Shanyang.
Looking about me at the bleak, wide fields,
I rest my carriage by the town-wall's corner.
Following the traces of these two men,
I come to their empty cottages by the narrow lane.

叹黍离之愍周兮,
悲麦秀于殷墟。

惟古昔以怀今兮,
心徘徊以踌躇。
栋宇存而弗毁兮,
形神逝其焉如?
昔李斯之受罪兮,
叹黄犬而长吟。
悼嵇生之永辞兮,
顾日影而弹琴。
托运遇于领会兮,
寄余命于寸阴。
听鸣笛之慷慨兮,
妙声绝而复寻。
停驾言其将迈兮,
遂援翰而写心。

I sigh over the "Drooping Millet" that laments the fall of Zhou,

and grieve at the "Blooming Wheat" that mourns the ruins of Yin.[1]

The ancient past stirs me to ponder the present,

I pace to and fro, hesitating in my heart.

The roofs and columns remain undamaged,

but where have their bodies and spirits gone?

Long ago, when Li Si was to meet his death,

he cried for the companionship of his yellow dog.[2]

I grieve that Master Ji has left me forever.

Looking back at his shadow and playing his zither,

leaving his fate to the turns of circumstance,

he entrusted his remaining life to that last inch of shadow.

I am moved by the singing of a flute,

its notes halting , then exquisitely continuing.

I halt my carriage before re-embarking on my journey,

and, taking up a brush, I let it convey my heart.

1　这两行分别引用了《诗经》和《史记》中的两个典故，其中涉及周、商两朝旧臣故地重游，凄怆感伤。These two lines contain two allusions, to *The Book of Poetry*, and the *Records of the Grand Historian*. In both cases, officials of the fallen Zhou and Shang dynasties visited the sites of the former dynasties and felt saddened.

2　李斯事见 153 页注。For Li Si, see the note on page 153.

刘 伶

Liu Ling

刘伶（？—？），字伯伦。初淡漠少言，鲜与人交，但与阮籍、嵇康相遇后，欣然神解，随即与他们携手进入竹林。他一生嗜酒，遗落世物，常携酒乘鹿车出游，使人荷锄随后，告其"死便埋我"。其《酒德颂》正体现了这一情怀。

Liu Ling (?–?), courtesy name Bolun, was said to be a quiet and aloof man, but when he met with Ruan Ji and Ji Kang, he experienced a spiritual rapport with them, and immediately followed them into the bamboo groves. All his life he was fond of drinking and showed no interest in the affairs of the world. One of his hobbies was to ride on a deer-driven cart with a jar of wine; when doing this he would ask someone to follow him with a shovel, and he would tell this person: "If I die, just bury me!" This life attitude is vividly described in his "Ode to the Virtue of Wine."

北芒客舍诗

泱漭望舒隐，
黮黤玄夜阴。
寒鸡思天曙，
拥翅吹长音。
蚊蚋归丰草，
枯叶散萧林。
陈醴发悴颜，
巴歈畅真心。
缊被终不晓，
斯叹信难任。
何以除斯叹？
付之与瑟琴。
长笛响中夕，
闻此消胸襟。

Sojourning at Beimang Mountain

The moon hides in the dim sky,

the night casts its black, gloomy shadows.

A cold rooster shivers and longs for daybreak,

it stretches its wings, uttering long cries.

Mosquitos and flies return to the thick grasses,

withered leaves are scattered through the desolate woods.

But old wine banishes my tired features,

and martial dances relieve my true heart.

Under a hemp cover I wait for the day to dawn,

these sighs of mine are hard to endure.

How may I dispel these sighs?

I pass them to my zither and lute.

A long flute sounds forth at midnight,

hearing this, my breast is cleared.

酒德颂

有大人先生者,
以天地为一朝,
万期为须臾,
日月为扃牖,
八荒为庭衢。
行无辙迹,
居无室庐,
幕天席地,
纵意所如。
止则操卮执觚,
动则挈榼提壶,
惟酒是务,
焉知其余?
有贵介公子,
搢绅处士,
闻吾风声,
议其所以。
乃奋袂攘襟,
怒目切齿,
陈说礼法,
是非锋起。
先生于是方捧罂承槽,

Ode to the Virtue of Wine

There lives a Great Master,

who regards both Heaven and Earth as a single morning,

myriad years as just one moment,

the sun and moon as door and window,

and the Eight Wildernesses merely courtyard and road.

He travels without leaving traces behind,

resides without a hut or room;

taking Heaven and Earth as curtain and mat,

he follows his heart wherever it leads.

Resting, he holds a goblet, grasps a cup,

on the move, he carries a jug or pot.

Wine is his only concern,

how would he care for anything else?

There's a man of noble birth

and a recluse, wearing his belt of office;

they, hearing the rumors about our Master,

venture to criticize his conduct.

They wave their sleeves, roll up their lapels,

glare angrily and grind their teeth,

expound on the rites and laws,

and argue with their spears the right and the wrong.

Upon this, the Great Master move his jar to the trough,

衔杯漱醪,
奋髯箕踞,
枕曲藉糟,
无思无虑,
其乐陶陶,
兀然而醉,
恍尔而醒。
静听不闻雷霆之声,
熟视不睹泰山之形,
不觉寒暑之切肌,
利欲之感情。
俯观万物,
扰扰焉如江汉之载浮萍。

二豪侍侧焉,
如蜾蠃之与螟蛉。

holds the cup to his mouth to savor his murky wine,
lets loose his hair and sits with his legs sprawled apart,
pillows his head on the foam, reclines on the lees,
and with no anxieties, no thought at all,
intoxicated with his pleasure,
now gets thoroughly drunk and lost,
then wakes up in forgetfulness.
Quietly listening, he is deaf to the sound of thunder,
looking intently, he can't see the bulk of Mount Tai.
He can't feel the cold and heat on his body,
nor sense the desire for profit and gain.
He casts a glance at the myriad things below,
how chaotic they are, like duckweed on the rivers of the
    Yangtze and the Han!
The two men swaggering, standing by his side,
look like mere flies and weevils.

译者简介

吴伏生，美国犹他大学中国文学及比较文学教授。著有专著 The Poetics of Decadence: Chinese Poetry of the Southern Dynasties and Late Tang Periods (1998)、Written at Imperial Command: Panegyric Poetry in Early Medieval China (2008)、《汉诗英译研究：理雅各、翟理斯、韦利、庞德》(2012)、《英语世界的陶渊明研究》(2013)、《中西比较诗学要籍六讲》(2016)，译有《迪伦·托马斯诗歌精译》(2014)，并发表有关中国文学、比较文学方面的论文多篇。

格雷厄姆·哈蒂尔，英国诗人，曾在南开大学、卡迪夫大学、斯旺西大学以及伦敦 Metanoia 学院讲授英国诗歌及诗歌创作。著有诗集 Ruan Ji's Island and (Tu Fu) in the Cities (1992)、Cennau's Bell (2005)、A Winged Head (2007) 和 Chroma (2013)，并发表有关社保、医护诗歌与文学创作方面的论文多篇。

此书为吴伏生与格雷厄姆·哈蒂尔合作翻译的第五本译作。此前他们还出版过《阮籍诗选英译》(1988，2006)、《曹植诗歌英译》(2013)、《三曹诗选英译》(2016)、《建安七子诗歌英译》(2018)。

About the Translators

Wu Fusheng is professor of Chinese Literature and Comparative Literary and Cultural Studies at the University of Utah. He is the author of *The Poetics of Decadence: Chinese Poetry of the Southern Dynasties and Late Tang Periods* (1998), *Written at Imperial Command: Panegyric Poetry in Early Medieval China* (2008), *A Study of English Translation of Chinese Poetry: James Legge, Herbert Giles, Arthur Waley and Ezra Pound* (2012), *Tao Yuanming Studies in the English-speaking World* (2013), *Selected Poems of Dylan Thomas* (2014), *Six Lectures on Key Works in East-West Comparative Poetics* (2016), as well as numerous articles on Chinese literature and comparative literature.

Graham Hartill is an English poet. He has taught English poetry and creative writing at Nankai University, Cardiff University, Swansea University, and for the Metanoia Institute, London. He is the author of several poetry collections which include *Ruan Ji's Island and (Tu Fu) in the Cities* (1992), *Cennau's Bell* (2005), *A Winged Head* (2007), *Chroma* (2013), as well as many essays on poetics and creative writing in social and health care settings.

This is the fifth collaborative work of Wu Fusheng and Graham Hartill. Previously they have also published English translations of the poetry of Ruan Ji (1988, 2006), Cao Zhi (2013), the Three Caos (2016) and the Seven Masters of the Jian'an era (2018).

中国古典文学英译丛书

《三曹诗选英译》

《建安七子诗歌英译》

《竹林七贤诗赋英译》

《孟浩然诗选英译》

《魏晋抒情赋英译》

《云室——一个英国人眼中的中国古诗》